SOAR
Your Blueprint for Holistic Success and Self-Mastery

Jim Hostler
The OM Coach

ISBN: 979-8-9903394-7-7

Library of Congress Control Number: 2024911714

Welcome

Welcome to the OM Spiritual Center, a sanctuary for people committed to transforming their human experience. I am honored to extend my heartfelt greetings to you as the founder of the OM Spiritual Center and the SOAR Institute for Holistic Living. You are embarking on a profound journey that empowers you to manifest anything your heart desires through the SOAR framework.

SOAR is not just a concept but a transformational blueprint for your life. It teaches you to rise above challenges, redefine success, and live from your inner wisdom. When followed, it enables you to create your life with purpose, prosperity, and fulfillment.

Think of SOAR as your fundamental foundation for life. This is what you will discover and learn:

Harness Your Inner Wisdom and Live from Your Soul Observer:
- This teaching guides you to cultivate a profound connection with your essence, enabling you to recognize and trust your innate inner wisdom. Living from your Soul Observer will unlock unparalleled clarity and unwavering conviction, allowing your true authentic self to be the ultimate source of your guidance.

Embrace Being Future-Focused and Be the Architect of Your Destiny:

- SOAR empowers you to transcend limiting beliefs and proactively shape your reality. You will learn to cultivate a vivid vision for your desired future, aligning your energy and actions with deliberate purpose, and propelling yourself toward fulfilling your dreams with unwavering certainty and velocity.

Live Your Life by the Principle of Altruistic Selfishness:

- Discover this revolutionary approach to contribution, rooted in the understanding that true, sustainable impact on the world flows from a place of personal fullness. By prioritizing your own well-being and growth, you cultivate a reservoir of energy and insight that allows you to give genuinely and abundantly, without depletion or resentment.

Transcend Traditional Success and Achieve Holistic, Purpose-Driven Success:

- Ultimately, SOAR provides the blueprint to integrate these powerful principles into every facet of your life. You will define and achieve success on your own terms, spiritual, emotional, mental, physical, and financial, cultivating a life of profound purpose, joy, and authentic contribution that resonates with your deepest truth.

SOAR is a journey that teaches you to illuminate your life and unlock your limitless potential. SOAR does not tell you what to do with your life, which is up to you, as you are the author of your life. Instead, it teaches you how to live guided by inner wisdom, a journey of evolving. Evolving is a journey to self-mastery.

The principles and teachings you will delve into are based on the philosophies of ontology and metaphysics. Ontology, the philosophy of being. We are human beings, not human doings or human havings. Metaphysics, beyond the physical. We are spiritual beings having a human experience, not humans with a soul. SOAR combines these two philosophies to create a multidisciplinary approach to achieve any result you want in your life. Blending their ancient wisdom and universal principles creates a transformative blueprint for your holistic success.

We are taught to relive our past countless times, hoping for something different to occur. We live from our past; from the stories we have told ourselves and the stories our culture and society have taught us. One of the fundamental teachings of SOAR, and a paradigm shift in how you live your life, is for you to live your life being future-focused. *Being future-focused unlocks your potential.* You live into your future life that you create, where your inner wisdom guides you. Now you *manage* how you relate to your past. This is a contextual shift and a significant element in holistic success.

Being future-focused and guided by your inner wisdom, intuition, and imagination moves mountains. This is how you create the life you have always dreamed of, and beyond.

Embrace the knowledge this book offers; consider it your guiding North Star. May SOAR be the catalyst for your profound metamorphosis, igniting the flames of your inner wisdom and creating your holistic success on your journey of evolving and self-mastery.

Namaste,

Jim Hostler
Founder, OM Spiritual Center
omspiritualcenter.com

Introduction

Note: *Please reference the SOAR model in the back of the book. The concepts and strategies presented in SOAR are based on this model. It serves as the foundation for everything discussed within these chapters, providing a visual roadmap for a transformational shift to occur in your life. I encourage you to reference this model as you read the book, using it as a guide to fully integrate the lessons, wisdom, and strategies offered.*

"Reality is created by the mind. We can change our reality by changing our mind" – Plato.

So begins your journey of SOARing in your life.

When faced with adversity or threats, eagles soar to greater heights to escape or evade their attackers. We can use the strategy of the eagle as a metaphor for SOARing to new heights, higher levels of consciousness, and success. Raising to higher levels of consciousness is your launching pad to all transformation in your life. Higher levels of consciousness cause you to seek new knowledge and gain access to new insights.

New knowledge and insights open the gates to envisioning and achieving new levels of success, your new levels of success as a natural reflection of who you are. You will learn to align your definition of success, the results you commit to, and the actions you take to achieve holistic success.

In our eagle metaphor, the eagle represents resilience, strength, and the ability to rise above challenges. Like the eagle rising to new heights, SOAR teaches you to rise into higher levels of consciousness... *no matter what happens in your outer world*. This is how you have the resilience, strength, and ability to overcome problems and challenges. This contextual shift in your life also guides you to see if the issue is still a problem or challenge, whether to have resilience and perseverance, or if you have transcended the issue.

With a view now from a higher perspective, you see new possibilities you previously could not see. Also, to be able to take new actions that you previously couldn't see. And now you accomplish new results you were incapable of, perhaps just a moment ago. Many of these results you previously resolved would forever be but hopes and dreams, believing there was no way you could ever accomplish them. Like the eagle, when you learn to SOAR, you can take your life to new heights where any dream can become a reality.

One fundamental element of SOAR is redefining success, from traditional to holistic success. Holistic success is living your life "inside out," where you create and design your life from your inner wisdom. It is living in connection with your soul, heart's wisdom, imagination, and intuition. It is success in all areas of your life and with all of life. It is success as you define it. This is living in harmony in your life. This is how you live a life with purpose and fulfillment. These are defining elements of transforming your life.

Another fundamental element and teaching of SOAR is to evolve in your life. To evolve is to raise your consciousness. And how do you evolve in life? The answer is in the word evolve: love is spelled backwards in evolve. To be loving, live connected to your heart's wisdom, live your life connected to your true authentic self, your essence, and listen to and honor your intuition and imagination.

Evolving in your life is a journey of self-mastery. And here is my favorite definition of a master:

"A master is a teacher who never stopped being a student." - unknown.

Being a master means being a lifelong student of your Self. This journey is on a path connected to your inner wisdom. But in today's egocentric and materialistic world, too few have this knowledge, and fewer live by it.

Note: *I use and define Self, with a capital "S," as defined in detail in the Hindu text, the Upanishads. The wisdom of the Self is through your heart. The ultimate goal is for us to rest in the knowing of our Self. Our Self is our ultimate spiritual Self. On this journey is our soul and higher self. I use soul and higher self to point to milestones on a spiritual journey to Self.*

SOAR is a holistic, multidisciplinary, fundamental foundation and transformative blueprint for your life. It allows you to be the architect of your destiny, regardless of your past. It is also experiential, allowing you to do and have anything you want.

Blessings on your journey to being able to take your life to new heights.

SOAR

SOAR is an acronym. It stands for success, observer, actions, and results. (A reminder for you to reference the SOAR model diagram at the back of the book.)

The model is comprised of four domains:

- **"S" stands for your success.** Success is defined as holistic rather than traditional. Holistic success is success from the inside out. Where you define and create your success from your true authentic self, what SOAR defines as your soul observer. You listen to and create your future life guided by your intuition and imagination. Imagination is what Neville Goddard refers to as Christ consciousness. I agree and use it in this context throughout the book. Holistic success is also having success and living in harmony in all areas of your life. Additionally, it is not something that defines you; rather, it is a reflection of who you truly are. It is who you are being and becoming.

- **"O," your observer self,** this is you. You as the observer of your life. Who you are, and the cause of your life, is given by either your ego or your higher Self, your soul. You, as your soul observer, is the very heart of SOAR. It is where you remain connected to and grounded in. It is what shapes the context of your life. Your inner world, the essence of your soul, the wisdom of your heart, and the power of your imagination and intuition fuel your ability to SOAR.

- **"A" is for the actions** you take to achieve your desired results that define your success. However, you will learn a transformational approach to why and when you take the actions you do. Instead of focusing on actions first and what to do, the action domain is your last domain to focus on and work in. You learn to first align yourself energetically to your divine wisdom. To then define your desired success and the results needed to achieve your success, *before taking any action.*

- The **"R" represents your Results.** The specific results you commit to fulfilling: your results commitments. Fulfilled results are your success. There is a powerful distinction between results commitments, and goals. Most goals are created from or given by outside influences and are task oriented. In contrast, when you commit to something, you are promising, declaring to yourself to fulfill your result. Commitments are made with a deep alignment with your soul observer and taking actions over time. Viewing goals and promises as energy, promises are higher energy than goals. As such, they are easier to keep and fulfill because they are in closer energetic alignment with your true self.

Although SOAR is an acronym, you don't apply it to your life in the S-O-A-R sequence. Rather, you use it in the sequence of O-S-R-A. Why? Because now you live your life inside-out. It is your true authentic self, your soul observer, that defines and guides your life. This is living connected to your divine wisdom. This also creates a fundamental foundation that you cannot outgrow because it is a reflection of your consciousness.

The transformative power of the SOAR model is that it is experiential and is meant to be lived.

It is a model, a transformational blueprint, for your life. When you embody learning the SOAR model, I promise it will transform your life. You will be able to obtain *any result,* anything you want to do or have, because you alter who you are.

What gives SOAR its uniqueness, holistic, and multidisciplinary approach so that you can transform your life and have any result you want? It is built on two cornerstones, two philosophies with ancient wisdom and universal principles. These two cornerstones are the philosophies of ontology and metaphysics. Ontology is the philosophy of being. We are human beings, not human doings or havings. And metaphysics is the philosophy beyond the physical.

We are spiritual beings having a human experience, not a human being with a soul.

Note: Ontology, the "O," and metaphysics, the "M," are the acronyms for the OM Spiritual Center, its core philosophies, and my life coaching. Ontology and Metaphysics are not abstract theories. They are blueprints infused with ancient wisdom and universal principles to transform your life.

These philosophies are the cornerstones for embarking on Socrates' profound quest to "know thyself." This is a journey to infinitely deepen and broaden your understanding of life. These two philosophies also lay the essential foundation for SOAR, encompassing a holistic (holy) approach that honors you as a spiritual being, a soul guided by your heart's wisdom, experiencing life through your body and emotions, and expressing yourself through language. Recognizing, nurturing, honoring, and integrating the whole person is fundamental to SOAR's multidisciplinary approach to transforming your life.

SOAR is you defining your success and aligning your thoughts, beliefs, feelings, behaviors, language, and actions to achieve the results that define your success *in all areas of your life.* Living inside-out, you will transform your life and transcend in consciousness, becoming a magnet for your desired results.

Material success and accomplishments will come if that is what you want. They are the effect of who you are, instead of you believing the outer world causes your success. You enjoy the material world without attachment or having it define you. This is holistic success, who you are, and who you are becoming.

A sidebar on non-attachment. Let me offer a compelling reason not to be attached to a desired outcome. You say you want "X," pick one of your result commitments (goals). Having created and defined it, you are acting in the spirit of success. You align with the fulfillment of your result before you take any action. Next, you use the power of language. As I teach in the *Life Vision to Mastery*[1] program, you complete each section of your life vision with, "And so it is (a declaration), this or greater!" Adding the "this or greater" is because your soul may have greater plans in store for you that today you cannot see. And as you rise in consciousness, what you think is your best today, you may discover is but a stepping stone to greater things in your life tomorrow. Always do your best, without attachment.

With you at the heart of SOAR, you know you always have the ability to choose who you are being. You are able, just like the eagle, to transform your life with your next breath and rise to new heights, higher levels of consciousness. And just like when an eagle is

---

[1] Life Vision to Mastery is a program offered through the OM Spiritual Center, omspiritualcenter.com.

attacked, it does not think about what to do next. It instinctively and intuitively knows how to climb fast to higher altitudes to escape its attacker. When faced with breakdowns, circumstances, situations, events, and people in your life that are challenging or disruptive to your energy, you will also know to raise your consciousness instinctively.

You have the power to decide who you are, who you are showing up as in your life, the thoughts you are having, and the beliefs you hold... always. Knowing that all your life reflects your level of consciousness, you hold the power to transform and transcend anything. To be able to, despite outside appearances and what is happening in the outer world, create anything you want in your life. And your life is always reflected in the frequency of your energy. It is the "vibe" you are showing up as in your life. An excellent analogy for how consciousness works is comparing consciousness to a radio. We all have used a radio. You tune into a radio station that is at a specific frequency. That radio station is playing a genre of music, or it is a talk show. You do not tune into a heavy metal radio station expecting Yanni or Enya to be playing on it. Nor do you dial into the classical radio station to get updates on sports.

Life works the same way. The frequency of our energy is reflected, *in its entirety,* in our reality.

This is precisely how our consciousness works. Consciousness is energy expressing at different frequencies. Think of the difference in the frequencies between blame, fear, resentment, anxiety, and joy, gratitude, compassion, and bliss. Feel the difference?!

Your life, everyone's life, is exactly the way it is, exactly the way it is not, because of the primary level of consciousness the person is living in. Period. End of story.

But what causes our primary level of consciousness? It is living our lives primarily focused on our past. We are taught to be past-focused. Our history and culture most often define who we are, what we do, our relationships, and our traditions. We are taught many things, and they are all stories made up from our past and accepted as the truth.

It is time to be a myth-buster in your life, to break the unconscious hold the past has on it, to know yourself, and to create your life regardless of your past.

Your thoughts and beliefs reflect your consciousness. It is your consciousness that defines the success you want in your life.

Your outer world is but a reflection of your inner world.

From consciousness to success, you are learning a transformational blueprint to do or have anything you want. And not just in one area of your life at the expense of others, but to have harmony in all areas of your life. This is why S-O-A-R is presented in the sequence of O-S-R-A. We will begin our journey with a deep understanding of yourself as the observer in your life. The observer domain comprises the multidimensional and holistic approach of SOAR. As the soul observer, you are the bedrock of your transformation and the cause of new levels of your success. Let us begin with the fundamental foundation for your life, to begin to know thyself.

Observer

At the heart of the SOAR model is you, as the observer of your life. It is who you are and how you perceive, make meaning, and interact with life. This defines how your life and the world occur to you. It filters and colors everything you encounter. Your observer self influences how you understand and interpret circumstances, situations, and events. It quite literally is in control of your thoughts, beliefs, feelings, language, emotions, body, and behaviors.

How you define yourself as the observer gives everything in and about your life. Everything!

The world appears uniquely to each individual because of our internal observer lens. This lens is influenced by your perceptions and perspectives, which give the context of your life. Your history and culture shape your perceptions and perspectives. As a result, no two people see the world the same way, leading to a rich diversity of viewpoints and understandings.

As your observer self, how you see or frame an occurrence creates the "starting point" for how you deal and interact with anything and anyone. How you interpret, perceive, listen, and speak affects your physical well-being and the emotions you experience. You establish the decisions, behaviors, and actions you will take, all of which set up the possibilities for the results you will get. The results you get are the level of success you achieve.

If you change the starting point, you change everything, including the possibilities of outcomes.

Few people realize this as they think that how they perceive things in life is the "way things are," "that is the way that it is," or that "it" is "the truth." Remember "the truth" is given by, based on, and created from the stories of your past. Many of these stories your ancestors told over possibly millennia have become ingrained in your culture.

You come to know that the "way things are," "that is the way it is," or "the truth," none of it is true. In fact, it could not be further from the truth. They are all made-up stories. Inherently, life has no meaning. Meaning is what we make it.

It is okay that they are stories, that is how humanity lives. This is a fundamental aspect of being human. Like all awareness, the power of this awareness is giving you a choice.

We choose to observe life through one of two domains. These domains are the starting points for what you do and what you have in life. They determine the outcomes of everything. These two observer domains are the **ego observer and the soul observer.**

This distinction, ego or soul, is the key defining point of SOAR. You are consciously determining, using your free will, who you are in your life. Is your life unconsciously given by, defined by, your egoic construct, your small, fear-based, decisive self, or are you consciously creating your life from your higher self, connected to your soul, and listening to your imagination and intuition? This distinction holds the power to alter your past, present, and future.

This is why I have said you are literally the heart of SOAR. This is because being connected to your soul observer is living your life through your heart's wisdom. Although the most common connection humanity is experiencing is to be connected to their *ego observer*. Here, you are not connected with your heart. Rather, it is the small mind, logic, divisiveness, competition, and fear-based egoic structure primarily, if not exclusively, running your life. In contrast is your *soul observer*. This is living being connected to your heart's wisdom, soul, intuition, and imagination.

Note: *If you want to look at the observer in another context, whether your ego or soul is in control, it is the strategic aspect of life. Actions would be our tactical aspect. But, as you are about to discover, most people focus solely on what actions they, or others, are going to take to get the desired results, ignoring the observer domain. Are you beginning to feel and understand the importance of the observer domain* *and what is missing when people focus solely on actions?*

Consciously choosing which observer you are being is knowing who you are giving control over your life to and who defines your life. It can only be your soul observer that defines and gives you holistic success with a future-focus.

It takes courage to become conscious of who you are as your observer self. To do this, you must bring the unconscious conscious. You must pause your life and look, feel, and reflect on who you are. This journey is beyond measure worth taking. I want to help you distinguish who your ship's captain is. Let's embark on further exploring and defining these two observer domains.

Ego Observer

The ego is the small, fear-based (false evidence appearing real), separate self. It is driven by fear and insecurity. It is these drivers that shape your perceptions and perspectives in life. When your egoic construct controls your life, it becomes the lens through which you view and interact with the world. It believes in competition and division and defines itself by associating with things, people, and material accomplishments. It loves to compare and judge. It seeks, sometimes outrageously, to defend and justify its beliefs. It is a master at comparing you with others to validate itself. It does this by seeking agreement with what others are saying, doing, or have. Its focus is on processes and what you are going to do. It has a deep attachment to external outcomes and no regard to who is doing the doing. These are the essence of the definition of traditional success.

The ego has three purposes for its existence:

- To predict
- To control
- To survive

All three of these are given by your past! Your ego always takes things from your past and places them into your future. This is unconsciously reliving life while believing great things are ahead for you. When you are living into what the ego has you believing is your future, you may change the people, places, or things, but you are reliving your past and calling it your future. Life becomes mostly habitual and lived from memory. This is your egoic construct using your history and culture to define your life. There is an element to this that is self-destruction. Self-destruction is because you are not connected to honoring and expressing your essence. You are closed to the divine flow of life.

When the ego takes the helm as the observer, success is defined by external markers like wealth, power, and fame. The ego observer can lead to success, but it often comes at the cost of inner peace, authenticity to one's true self, and almost always a lack of true and fulfilling purpose. Success given by the egoic construct is not holistic success. Egoic success lacks soul, quite literally.

Take a moment to reflect: When was the last time you made a decision from fear or judgment? How might this decision have differed if guided by your intuition or imagination?

Soul Observer

In complete contrast to the ego observer is the soul observer. This is living "inside-out," guided by your inner wisdom, and connected to your higher self, your soul. You consciously live your life as your essence, your true authentic self. This is being connected to the wisdom of your heart, intuition, and imagination.

This is where your transformation begins. Your intuition and imagination are the core to connecting to your soul, which allows you to see, feel, and envision your new levels of holistic success. Through this wisdom, you create your life (we are infinite spiritual beings, co-creators with Source). This is you living life from higher consciousness.

However, since the Scientific Revolution in the 17th century, we have been taught to turn off, suppress, and ignore our intuition and imagination. Here is another part of the ignorance of our history and culture. It is time to complete our ignorance and open ourselves to divine wisdom. To allow our intuition and imagination to guide us in our lives. They are inherently part of our essence; it is time to be true to ourselves.

Who you have created yourself to be in life likely has been an unconscious way of being your whole life. It is for most of us, until it is not. Back to our history and culture defining our lives. It is time to bring awareness to the fact that humanity has, and is living, an unsustainable path. We have taken ourselves to a crisis in every domain of our lives. Every domain. What is needed, and I believe is happening in our world today, is a revolution of consciousness. When humanity raises their consciousness, living as their soul observer being in control of their lives, we will live in a new world. SOAR is a blueprint for this to happen.

As Gandhi said, and it has never been more needed than today, "If you want to change the world, start with yourself."

Consciously transforming the focus in your life is a deliberate process. Humanity has a long history of being the ego observer. But with conscious effort, it is time to transform ourselves into living as the soul observer. As the soul observer, everything changes in your life. Or, more accurately stated, the context of your life transforms. And along with transformation comes transcendence.

There are three cornerstones to living as a soul observer. As the name states, you live connected to and guided by your inner wisdom, your soul. This connects you to your first cornerstone, your intuition and imagination, which become your guides. Next, you are altruistically selfish. Third, you live your life being future-focused instead of reliving your past.

Guided by your inner wisdom, free of the constraints of cultural and societal narratives and expectations, begins your journey of freedom.

Living in states of higher consciousness means riding up in your mood elevator to higher states of emotions and moods. For example, you live in joy, peace, happiness, compassion, excitement, and an inner calm grounded in certainty. You align your emotions to living your life with a deep sense of alignment with your virtues.

You are also living your life with contentment. This is the domain of "peace beyond understanding," liberation, and freedom. Now guided by your inspiration (in-spirit), have all the success you want in life. However, being holistically successful is not success at the expense of other areas of your life, others, or nature.

Being peaceful and knowing thyself, you shift how you deal with the outside world and with others. This is especially true when something isn't working out or there is a breakdown. Now, grounded and centered in your soul observer, you know to *respond* into the world and never *react* to the world. And when you respond, you are now responding in higher levels of consciousness, ever mindful that your actions are purposely taken.

Next is where real transformation and magic happen. Being open and in higher consciousness, you connect to and develop your intuition and imagination. Your intuition is the inner voice that is always available to you. But it does not compete for space. If you are tuned into your ego and the cacophony in our outer world, it is not to be heard. Be still and know, listen. It is the wisdom of your soul speaking to you. This is where you know, and you know you know. It is a connection to deeper, inner wisdom that transcends conscious reasoning. It is direct insight and understanding that guides you in your decisions and how you stay true to your authentic self. It often speaks to you as a "gut feeling" or a sense of certainty without needing logical or material evidence. This is where your soul gives you advice to guide you because it can see "behind the veil" of what the material world is showing you. It sees the truth and aligns you to your true purpose and the greater flow of life. Doubt, fears, and uncertainties vanish. Being intuitive is a natural aspect of who we all are.

You also get access to your imagination playing a larger role in your life. Intuition is more of your reasoning essence, whereas imagination is the divine creative juices to life. It is one of the most profound expressions of your essence. It is your connection to higher levels of consciousness, a connection to your higher self, Christ consciousness. Intuition and imagination are sacred bridges between our inner and outer worlds. Imagination is a powerful ingredient, if not often the source, to manifesting in your life. It isn't going to show you something unless you are capable of its fulfillment... let that sink in!

Imagination is a force that creates new realities in your life. It allows you to step into new possibilities and turn these possibilities into new realities, regardless of how or what your life is like today. When you transform who you are and align with your higher self, Christ consciousness, you access higher versions of yourself. You are bringing this new version of yourself into the present reality of your life; it is who you are and who you are becoming.

A Note on this last statement. Who you are and who you are becoming is a common understanding of evolving. Rather, you are already a perfect expression of your essence, your divine self, we all are. So, it is not a place to get to, but it is a place we already infinitely are. It is a place to remember. But it is humanities journey in the egoic construct that has created stories over millennia, which has caused separation from our essence. In truth, we are not evolving to higher consciousness expressing in our lives; rather, we are removing the roadblocks we have both inherited and created in our lives to be able to experience our true essence. When you heal a hurt, you remove a roadblock to experiencing higher states of consciousness. When you heal past trauma, breakdowns, the stories of lack, limitation, and "I'm not worth it" handed down from generations, all of this and more, you are removing the roadblocks to you being able to experience more connection to your true essence: your divine self in your human experience. We are all made in the image and likeness of God: divine, infinite creators. Transcending our egoic construct allows you to experience more of your true authentic self. This is mastery-level knowledge in the domain of self-mastery.

Imagination deals with the potential of your material reality and what is possible in your life. It shows you, grounded in your thoughts, desires, and results commitments, what your true authentic spiritual self is capable of that has yet to manifest into your reality. Imagination is your insight into your future self, where you turn what you imagine into your reality.

It is most often your imagination that evokes your passion, inspiration, excitement, and similar high-level emotions and moods. These emotions are proof of your connection between your soul and your physical reality. Connected to your soul is the level of your consciousness that you have to be in to feel these emotions. And you also feel them because they are the bridge between your soul and the actions you take to get the outcomes you want in life. This bridge is your soul confirming you are in alignment with your truth. This is why you are feeling these higher-level emotions. This is the energy in which you create and live your authentic life.

Developing your intuition and imagination opens you to your essence. They are powerful and transformative because they are inherently an aspect of your true authentic self, your heart's wisdom, your soul.

Our next cornerstone of the soul observer is to be altruistically selfish in your life. You cannot give unless your cup is running over. Knowing thyself, which aligns with the first three domains of your life vision in the *Life Vision to Mastery* program, you define yourself. But life isn't happening in a vacuum.

As you give, you get, a Law of the Universe. As you define your results commitments, you interact and need help from others. This is why SOAR defines money as help. You create your success, and an element of that has a financial component to it. You need to make money to fulfill your results commitments. Only with SOAR, you are being altruistically selfish, primarily to fulfill your financial commitments.

You now help others fulfill their results commitments, an altruistic element, and by helping them, you are also being compensated, a selfish element. We help each other fulfill our results commitments. You "win," I "win," and the person buying or benefiting from the goods or services being provided "wins." You live to be of service; however, your being of service also fulfills your results commitments and your holistic success.

This, too, is living with a pay-it-forward mindset. A critical note about this mindset: do not be attached to how or from whom you receive. The universe in its divine intelligence always balances the books. You don't give to receive. This is the paradox of this law. If you give from a place of expectation to receive, that is doing it from a lack mentality, of which the universe will provide more of it to you, and manipulation. You are trying, by giving, to manipulate the outcome.

Explained slightly differently, being altruistically selfish is being other-centric or people-centric. It is living with a mindset of service. When you define your purpose and then serve others through your purpose, this is the highest calling we have as humans.

What are you connected to, your egoic construct or your higher self? And as you consciously exercise this choice, there will come a time when who you are is an expression of your higher self, your soul. You have transcended choice and become a being of higher consciousness. At this level of life, you no longer have to choose between ego or soul, as you become an embodiment of your higher self. It becomes who you are. This is how and when you are living your life inside-out.

This is self-mastery.

We live in the eternal now. In the present is life. But with the seduction and habitual way of being that the egoic construct creates for us, it is hard to break the chains to the past. It is hard not to have your past controlling your life. But in the present, you can always connect to guidance from your intuition and imagination. But then what?

Do you return to old familiar ways and habits, and resolve that the inspiration you just tapped into was a fleeting dream? Or do you stay connected to your divine wisdom, and instead of allowing past habits to control you, you shift to being future-focused? To create your life free of the constraints of the past?

This brings us to our third element of the soul observer, which is to be future-focused.

Future-Focused

What direction is your life focused, toward the past or the future?

We all know the only reality is the infinite, fleeting, present. Eckhart Tolle's famous book *The Power of Now* taught us this. But this is part of the equation. Sure, being present when you are meditating or praying is the only way they are going to happen. Being present when we are totally into something, professional athletes call this the zone, serves as another example. Consciously connected to your soul observer causes you to be in the present. Being in the present is the only "place" in which life happens. It is the only place reality exists.

What happens when you step out into life? Being consciously in the present, your forever question is "What direction am I focused in my life?"

Only in the present can we connect to our divine creative power. Where you express yourself as your true authentic self. And where you are in your power to consciously choose what your tomorrows will be.

With no conscious awareness of how to be present and what direction you are pointing in life, your ego has you. Your ego plays a unique hand in crafting your life. It is a master at creating your life based on your history and culture. It takes circumstances, situations, and events from your past and puts these things in your future, and then has you believe you are living a nice life, living into your future. It also looks for things in the past, with others, to verify and justify that things are the way they are today. When, in reality, this causes you to live into your future given by your past. Sounds a little like a carousel... because it is. Your ego is a master in this domain, and it takes a conscious effort, over time, with many insights, to break its chains.

Remember, humanity is primarily living unconsciously from their egoic construct. And just a reminder, the egoic construct has three purposes:

- To control
- To predict
- To survive

The egoic mind is a past-focused mechanism. It thrives on identity shaped by past experiences and inherited narratives, which create our cultures and traditions.

Speaking of traditions, here is my favorite definition: a tradition is allowing your ancestors to control your future.

And now the stage is set. The stage is the narratives created from our stories. They become the narratives of our lives. Yet we forget these narratives are stories and live as though they are the truth. Being present allows you to deconstruct stories from your past. To uncover the birth and meaning of the stories that define your life and why they hold the meaning for you that they do. This becomes a conscious effort to break the cycles of the past, reliving past stories, traditions, and wounds. To break the illusion of forward motion and progress in our lives. Because your reality, your tomorrow, has been unconsciously defined by your past. And you are calling it your future.

Living by reliving your past is living a life defined mainly by hopes, dreams, and desires without the awareness and skills necessary to fulfill them. It is setting yourself up, mostly, if not entirely, and unconsciously, for a false future. "Ya, that would be nice," or "I hope so" are familiar narratives in this domain. You hope for a better future while remaining tethered to the past. Lack, limitations, problems, and challenges persist.

This is a repetition of patterns disguised as progress. Changes are made, with different people and new technologies, but these changes are not transformations. They are repeating past patterns, hoping for a new future. And there may be a deeper reason for operating in life this way.

Our deep-seated fears and uncertainties of yesterday often keep us trapped in our familiar and known reality. This stagnates and limits our lives, preventing us from being authentic to ourselves and truly being creators. It isn't until and unless you face a breakdown greater than your fears and uncertainties that you look for new ways to be different, to move beyond today's comforts, and change and transform your life.

You transform your life by bringing awareness to how your history, culture, traditions, and individual and societal narratives unconsciously define and control it. Now, you can see the limitations of unconsciously living your life.

This is your portal to creating a new life. You can only change anything in the present. Being present and reflecting on your past, you can learn from it and take its lessons. You can also recontextualize the past, using it to support your future success.

This is a great time to pause and reflect on your problems, challenges, and recurring issues that stop or limit your success. Now, in the present, and as your soul observer, you must uncover their root cause.

- What emotions keep surfacing that draw you back to relive your past?

- Scan your body. Any tightness or sensations you feel when you think about these things? What is your body wanting to tell you?
- Think about your language. What narratives do you find yourself repeating? How is this keeping you tied to your past?

This is awareness and your invitation to step out of the cycle of repeating your past. You will still want to have elements, perhaps many of them, of your past in your life. But they no longer unconsciously control your life. Instead, you will consciously manage how you have them in your life.

Your new awareness continues to unfold. What do you do if your past no longer controls your life? Not yet. The primary cause of transforming your life isn't about first focusing on what actions to take or what to do. This is the reaction almost everyone has initially. *Instead, it is about who you are, in the present.* It is connecting to the portal to infinite potential: the eternal present moment and your essence. Being in the present is your access to your self-empowerment.

Using your emotions, create yourself into a higher emotional state, such as gratitude or compassion. Notice how your body and emotions align with your higher emotional state. This helps and supports you in being present and staying future-focused.

In the present is where you hear your intuition and feel your imagination. Be still and listen.
You may want to engage in meditation or breathwork to center yourself. Journaling is another way to center yourself and connect with your essence. These connect you to your divine wisdom. This, too, is the place for insights to be given to you.

In the present, you feel and know if you are repeating past patterns or intentionally creating your life and breaking free of past challenges and limitations.

This is where you become present to who is choosing your thoughts, emotions, feelings, language, and actions. Is it your ego observer or your soul observer?

In the present, being your soul observer unlocks you from the shackles of your past. Your soul now becomes your compass. Guided by your intuition and imagination, you are tapped into the infinite field of possibilities. As you strengthen your soul observer, you strengthen your connection to your higher self.

This is where you transform and transcend yourself from being past-focused, repeating the cycles of your past, to being future-focused. This is where you respond into life, divine creator.

Where life happens through you, not to you.

Future-focused is what unlocks your potential. You tap into and define your potential guided by your imagination and intuition. Now, in higher consciousness, you can see beyond today's circumstances. You can envision any future you want for yourself, regardless of how your life is currently or was in the past.

Einstein gave us a glimpse of the importance of imagination when he said, "Imagination is more important than knowledge."

Centered in the present, future-focused, living your life as your soul observer, and being altruistically selfish. The cornerstones to build any life you want are now set.

You live into your future guided by your divine wisdom. Your intentions, purpose, and actions are all directed at the fulfillment of what you create for your future self. Your future self that you, in the present, are always living into.

You may think I am making your past wrong? Not at all. Instead, you recontextualize your relationship with your past. Bring as much or as little of your past into your life. Use it to build your future, no right or wrong, but rather awareness. But by consciously becoming aware of and recontextualizing your past, you break the cycle of repeating it. You now consciously use your past to help and support you in creating your future. Again, your future that you are always divinely guided to be creating in the infinite present.

Be in the present, being future-focused.

As within, so without.

Becoming and being future-focused is a holy journey where every aspect of your life reflects your soul's purpose. It is not a destination but rather a dynamic unfolding of your life. Being future-focused also gives you the freedom to create a life where anything is possible.

This is your journey to living a fulfilling life with purpose, to being on a path of evolution to self-mastery.

Your knowledge deepens.

Increased knowledge gives you access to greater insights. I want to offer a moment to reflect on SOAR's teachings.

- You have learned the structure of SOAR.

- We have redefined success to be holistic.

- SOAR is built on the cornerstones of the philosophies of Ontology and Metaphysics.

- Life is a journey of evolving.

- Evolving to self-mastery. *The wisdom of the Self is through your heart.*

- You are the heart of SOAR, as it is your connection to divine intelligence, with your intuition and imagination as your guides.

- Your life becomes future-focused instead of recycling the past.

I invite you to reflect on these teachings to deepen and help you embody this new knowledge and integrate new insights. I offer additional questions to help you understand the material better.

- How has your understanding of success shifted since redefining it as holistic?

- Are your current goals aligned with this new definition, or are old paradigms pulling you back?

- Holistic success isn't just about what you have, it is about who you are and who you are becoming. How does this resonate with you? What is coming up for you regarding your success?

- When you think about your life as a journey of evolving, where do you feel most called to grow right now?

- Evolving and growth are not a destination but a way of being.

- How connected do you feel to your intuition and imagination?

- When did you last act on a strong intuitive "hit" or an insight from your imagination?

- Are your current actions aligned with creating a future-focused life, or do you notice patterns of recycling your past?

- How deeply have you embraced the idea that YOU are the heart of SOAR?

- Do you recognize your innate power to transform your reality?

Each of these questions and statements holds a gateway to your next breakthrough. As you reflect on them, be open and curious. SOAR isn't just a philosophy; it's a lived experience. Experienced in all areas of your life and reflecting your consciousness.

This is why you can never outgrow SOAR as your transformational blueprint for your life.

I invite you to begin to anchor being future-focused by writing a letter to your future self. Please describe, in detail, who you want to become, what your life looks like, and how it feels. What one action can you take today to fulfill this vision?

With greater knowing, focus, clarity, and direction, our SOARing journey continues.

Transformational Action Steps

SOAR is an experiential and transformational blueprint for your life, but it only works if you work it. Introducing new knowledge into your life creates new paradigms and contexts from which to create and live. You will also gain new insights along the way. SOAR can seem overwhelming initially. I want to offer some action steps to help and support you on your transformational journey. Use these to help you anchor SOAR into your life.

Note: *Before you dive into these steps, please be in the emotional state of being curious, open, and wonder, with the mindset of a beginner.*

Self-Awareness: Continuously monitor your thoughts, feelings, emotions, body, and language (internal and external) to ensure they align with your higher self, intentions, virtues, and life vision. Bringing the unconscious conscious, awareness, is the beginning of all transformation in life.

Self-Reflection: This goes beyond the traditional glancing in the rearview mirror of life. One aspect of self-reflection is to be able to know yourself better and to define what really matters to you. What do you care most about? What inspires you? Your soul knows, intuition tells you, and imagination shows you. Another area to apply self-reflection to is a problem or challenge, current or anything from your past, that you are facing. Whatever you focus on, be with it. Combine journaling and prayer with it. Take time to reflect and get to the root cause of why it is a problem or a challenge. They always come with a lesson. In your self-reflection, take time to find the lesson. What gift does it hold for you? What is it wanting to teach you? Reflect to clarify why you want, or have, "that" in your life. Finding the root cause of your problems and challenges allows you to reframe, heal, transform, and transcend them. The power of self-reflection! Do not underestimate it.

Set Intentions: Intentions are powerful transformers for your life. This is using generative language to create what you want in your life. Setting intentions daily or for projects is excellent on a micro level. On a macro level, utilizing intentions within your life vision is where your life's power is clarified and defined. This is what supercharges your dreams into reality. Intentions bring focus and context to what matters and what you care about most.

Mindfulness: Practice mindfulness to stay present and make conscious decisions. This helps you act in alignment with your higher self. The connection to your soul, intuition, and imagination only occurs in the present. Equally important to being present is the direction your life is focused. Again, be mindful to be in the present while being future-focused, which causes radical transformation in your life. And when you are not present, know that your ego has taken control of your life. When this happens, breathe, reconnect to your soul, and being future focused.

Journaling: Is a powerful way to transcend the egoic construct and connect with your soul. It allows you to get out of your way, to go deeper, and connect with your divine wisdom. Write yourself into connection with your heart's wisdom, transcending your egoic construct. To be able to hear your intuition. I promise journaling will give you new insights and awareness to help and support you on your new journey of SOARing in your life.

Meditation: The sages and gurus of antiquity knew the power of meditation thousands of years ago. Developing your ability to meditate often takes time to quiet the ego's insatiable need for noise… self-talk. But beyond the ego's noise is the realm of the divine, the infinite, and the realms of higher consciousness. This is where you gain access to the wisdom of your soul and profound insights to apply to your life.

Prayer: While meditation is being open and allowing wisdom to come, prayer is asking for something. You often come to prayer with intention. And while there are many ways to pray, affirmative prayer, affirming you have the results you want before you begin to pray, is the most powerful way to pray. Thanking God for already having what you say you want. You are a divine creator, own it. Then allow, get out of your way (your ego), and let God show you the way. This is having faith. This is being a co-creator in manifesting your holistically successful life.

Remember, the observer domain of SOAR is your inner world, the heart of your life, and SOAR. When you are connected to and grounded in your soul observer, you ignite your path to your holistic success.

When you begin to take these transformational action steps and practice them daily, you will begin to open to your inner world, your true authentic self. Your intuition will become stronger. Your imagination will become brighter. You will start to overcome today's problems and challenges while creating and fulfilling new results commitments for yourself. Fulfilled results commitments are the stepping stones to your higher levels of holistic success. Holistic success is lasting success.

But your journey of SOARing is about to become exponentially stronger. When you embark on and travel the journey of raising your consciousness, evolving in your life, and being committed to your self-mastery, you create a level of self-empowerment that is beyond your capacities today.

Add POWER to Your Success

In his classic book, *Power vs. Force,* Dr. David Hawkins explores the distinction between two types of energy that influence our behavior: power and force. They are often used interchangeably, but they are worlds apart. Force is derived from low levels of consciousness, such as fear, anger, shame, anxiety, greed, and manipulation. Police and military are forceful, not powerful. Power is derived from higher states of consciousness such as joy, peace, truth, gratitude, and compassion. Dr. Hawkins emphasizes that true power, rooted in integrity and alignment with universal truth, has a far more profound and lasting effect than force, which is coercive and unsustainable.

SOAR, as a transformational blueprint for your life, would not be complete without an element of self-empowerment. Your journey to and living in holistic success is a journey of evolving. This is a journey of your life being aligned with your soul. This is a journey of living and experiencing life in higher states of consciousness. A natural out picturing of higher states of consciousness is authentic self-empowerment.

Authoring your holistic success, you do so by being connected to your inner wisdom, again, this occurs in higher levels of consciousness. This is the very essence of creating your holistic success versus chasing after traditional success. You transcend the expectations and definitions of traditional success.

Your journey to obtaining new levels of success is primarily defined by the new knowledge you acquire and the new insights you gain. Insights are not something in your outer world to find. Rather, they reside with your connection to the divine wisdom within you. Remember, it takes new knowledge *and* new insights to get new results. The power of SOAR is that the new insights you obtain come from your heart's wisdom, your intuition, and your imagination. Who you become is someone living their life from universal truth.

Yes, you may get new technology and systems, work with different people, etc., much like trying to do something different on the journey of traditional success. But with holistic success, you have altered the context in which you do the doing. Said differently, you altered who is doing the doing, who you are that is taking actions. Connected to your soul observer and utilizing SOAR's multidisciplinary approach, you now operate with a tremendous amount of Self-em-power-ment. Your self-empowerment is not the egoic journey of power, money, and fame that traditional success often seeks. Rather, your success is now about having purpose and fulfillment in life. You are now creating your outer world as a reflection of your inner world, which is a lifelong, evolving journey. Evolving is evolving into self-mastery.

This will enable you to achieve holistic success in ways and levels you cannot see or envision today.

You can only see and envision your future from the level of consciousness you are in today. Raise your consciousness, transform, and transcend as your observer self, and you alter your life views. *You alter the starting point of everything you do in your life.*

For example, if you are in the mood of blame and victim, you can only see, in traditional success, as far as a person stuck in blame and feeling like a victim can see. Which, to say the least, is not very far!

Note: I say traditional success because of the low-energy emotions. These are ego emotions, not higher-level emotions associated with the soul observer.

Conversely, when you are in a mood of gratitude and compassion and forward-focused in your life (remember, forward vision unlocks your potential!), you can envision a completely different landscape filled with new possibilities and opportunities.

Note: As your soul observer, you are only capable of higher-level emotions. When you are your soul observer, you transcend the low-vibration emotions of the ego observer. This is a creative force for your holistic success.

But this awareness is only the beginning of your journey. This journey of evolving and self-mastery will cause you to seek, become aware of, and fulfill new levels of success that you cannot currently imagine. When you live as your observer self, you gain new awareness, knowledge, and access to new insights. These are extraordinarily powerful transformers for your life and will have you redefining your success. You will also have to redefine your results commitments to align with your new definitions of success. Remember, your fulfilled results commitments give, define, and allow you to achieve your holistic success. This, in a nutshell, is the path of self-mastery. Understanding power, as Dr. Hawkins defines it, your SOARing journey now becomes one of self-empowerment.

I invite you to take a few deep breaths before reading the following description of self-empowerment. They are a reflection of your life when you show up in your greatness with humility, honoring your true authentic self.

The following is what will happen, what you will experience, what you will feel and do, as you live your life as your soul observer.

To you, mine, and humanity's self-empowering journey. Here lies the journey of self-empowerment: Your first step is to

- Raise your consciousness.

Connect to your inner world, your heart's wisdom, listening to your intuition and imagination. Be still and listen. Evolving into higher states of consciousness, you alter who you are. You alter your experience of life. Whether you call this Brahman realization, Christ consciousness, enlightenment, or journey to Self, this is where this path leads you. Higher consciousness has the power to recode your DNA. It alters who you are and who you are becoming. It is rebirthing yourself into a higher consciousness being. This causes you to alter, sometimes radically, internal elements of your life. This is where the epiphanies of insight come from. This is the journey of evolution. And evolution is the journey to self-mastery.

This is the revolution of consciousness the world so desperately needs today.

I promised you that SOAR was a transformational blueprint and a multidisciplinary approach to your holistic success. The pinnacle of the multidisciplinary approach is the self-empowerment element. Remember, SOAR is experiential; you have to act on the teachings. Raising your consciousness means you are now adding the element of authentic self-empowerment to your life.

Again, I invite you to take a moment and be with this teaching. Let your soul speak to you and feel its transformative and transcendent power for your life.

Now, in who you are, in ever-evolving higher levels of consciousness, this is what is guaranteed to happen in your life:

You will experience:
- new perceptions
- new perspectives
- new thoughts
- new beliefs
- new insights
- new intentions
- new distinctions
- new emotions
- new moods
- new feelings
- new language
- new ambitions
- new behaviors
- new practices

To have you take:
- new actions

You will also have:
- improved physical well-being and vitality.
- a deeper sense of who you are, to know thyself.
- increased confidence.
- transcended problems and challenges.
- raised your Emotional Intelligence.

You will also:
- develop new concerns in your life.
- change what you care most about in your life.
- live your life with purpose.
- live a fulfilling life.
- have better focus on what actions to take.
- have more clarity on how to take action.
- have a clearer sense of direction for your life.
- operate with velocity in life.
- live co-creating your life with the Multiverse.
- live being future-focused.

This is your authentic, self-empowered self that all humans are designed for. This is the self-empowered self you are and are always becoming, which enables you to define and have holistic success and fulfill your results commitments. Fulfilled results commitments are your success. Again, this is not some arbitrary thing you plug into your outer world. This is your true authentic self, soul, expressing, creating, designing, and causing your life. This is you being the architect of your destiny, accomplishing any level of holistic success you desire.

And your success that you author and define… get present to how much self-empowerment you now have access to. To be able to fulfill your dreams and desires, not only to have holistic success but also to take your success to any level you want to.

Awe... the power of new knowledge in your life! Now imagine the new insights waiting for you when you begin bringing this new knowledge into your life!

Your access to self-empowerment occurs because you did not ask yourself, "What am I going to do?" Instead, you asked yourself, "Who am I?" This is the unfoldment of the infinite quest to know thyself.

Transformational!

Transcendent!

We must return to the emotion domain to continue augmenting our transformational journey of success.

Learning in the observer domain requires you to learn the advanced skill of intentionally setting and holding your emotions before you embark on learning. To create yourself to be open, curious, and compassionate. In the Bible, Jesus says that to enter the kingdom of heaven, people must change and be like children. Why do you think he said that? Children are open and curious. They have no attachment to things. And perhaps most importantly, children are humble. True success has no room for hubris. No one is taking your beliefs or values from you, put them aside for a minute and explore a new domain of learning with your mind like a child... regardless of your level of experience or education.

Humility is a superpower.

In today's fast-paced, "I want it now" world, gaining new knowledge and skills takes time. Understanding this helps and supports you on your journey. Let's look at the levels of learning and competence you go through on your journey to self-mastery.

Levels of Learning and Competence

A fundamental principle of SOAR is that new knowledge is needed to achieve new results. Knowledge is gained by learning things from the outside world, and it exists whether you know about it or not.

Note: This section deals only with acquiring new knowledge and not gaining new insights. Insights are gained from your connection with your intuition and imagination. Insights are born from your inner world. As such, they happen outside our time and space, where epiphanies happen. When you tap into universal consciousness, divine wisdom, God only knows what wisdom you will gain. Insights cause us to alter who we are, often causing a shift in our consciousness, as they are subjective, internal, and generative. Knowledge usually does not alter your consciousness. Insights are one aspect of our learning journey; knowledge is the other.

Milestones mark the path of self-mastery. These milestones are levels of learning and competence achieved on your journey to self-mastery. Self-mastery, remember, is to know thyself. These levels of learning and competency are universal.

Although the following levels of learning and competence are universal, I invite you to learn and apply them in the context of knowing thyself. This is an infinite journey within. The journey of knowing thyself leads to self-mastery, to be the master of your life. I want to offer you my favorite definition of a master:

A master is a teacher who never stops being a student.

According to A Course in Miracles, we are always learning and teaching. This is another fundamental element of life.

Knowing the following six levels of learning and competence to become a master of your life helps with your patience to learn. Not having patience is a form of arrogance. Your ego is controlling your life if you lack patience. The journey of self-mastery is a dance between knowing how to have perseverance and patience.

Where do we begin our learning journey? Let's start with the largest domain of knowledge, what we don't know that we don't know. Despite our vast and ever-increasing amounts of knowledge, this is still the largest domain of knowledge. So, the first domain of learning and competence is **ignorance**. We simply do not know, despite our level of consciousness, there is still so much we do not know. This is especially true if someone is locked into their egoic construct and not open. They unconsciously go through life ignorant that life could be any different.

But with the awareness of our ignorance, we have our first choice point. We can choose to stay ignorant, many people do, or we can advance to our second level of learning and competence, that of a **beginner**.

With the desire to escape ignorance, our journey of acquiring new knowledge begins. We all begin our learning and competence journey as beginners. Opening to learning something new often starts with a feeling that something is missing or a nagging sense of unfulfillment, regardless of material wealth. This is also true irrespective of how much education, skills, or success you currently have. Often, the challenge is to be open and not collapse or compare what you already know with what you are taking on to learn. There are advantages to comparing in our learning journey, just be mindful of when and how you do it. With all new learning, you gain new competencies and skills. As a beginner, you are not proficient in any competence or skill, which comes with time and practice. It takes time to learn new things. It is also noteworthy to remind ourselves that we learn from our mistakes. This is your invitation to stay open and be patient with yourself. Consistency in obtaining results will come, but not in the beginner domain.

Our next step in learning is becoming an **advanced beginner**. This is where we start to produce consistency in our results. Mistakes become fewer, and often, mistakes made become bigger learning and growth opportunities. There are areas within our new learning domain where we begin to feel comfortable. Obtaining a certain comfort level in our new knowledge and getting consistency in results calls for a reminder to keep and maintain our humility on our learning journey.

This is the perfect time to begin working with a coach or teacher on your learning journey.

You are advancing far enough on your new learning journey to become more proficient in closing the gap between concept and the practical application of your learning. Getting a coach or teacher now is the perfect time because they do not have to spend an inordinate amount of time teaching you what to learn. Instead, they can focus on helping and supporting you to achieve your desired results.

As all learning takes practice, the coach or teacher also guides you in the proficiency of your knowledge, bringing depth to your learning to augment your learning path. Also, they make sure you are practicing your new skill correctly. Imagine practicing and getting really good at the wrong thing! Getting good at the wrong things quickly leads to breakdowns and a dead end on your journey to success. Finally, a coach or teacher adds an element of accountability to your learning.

Progressing on our learning journey. As our knowledge and skills become better, we become

competent as learners. What we have learned becomes automatic for us. We are embodying our learning at this level of learning. Our new knowledge and skills are getting "out of our heads" and becoming a natural picturing of who we have become. Think about when you learned to drive a car. After a little while, you did not have to think about what you needed to do to safely drive the car down the highway. Now we are consistently achieving our desired results. At the competence level of learning, we have also become good at anticipating and dealing with problems.

Practice, practice, practice, coupled with time, and we become a **virtuoso**. We are seen as excellent within our area of knowledge. We now bring "our style" to the table. No pun intended, but learning to be a chef is an example. Our level of learning has brought us to the point of being able to add, modify, edit, and individualize what we now know. This is where we may begin to bring in a level of creativity to the subject. Reliable consistency in our results commitments occurs. Said differently, we are consistently successful… at this level of success.

Mastery

Self-mastery, to know thyself, is the ultimate goal of life. But mastery has no summit, for once you arrive at a summit, you discover countless more. This is the ever-evolving aspect of life. But at this level of learning, you have taken in learning from others only to shed everything and become true to yourself. Sounds a little like an oxymoron, but it isn't. Think of the Olympic athletes. Extreme training and practicing, but in the end, they must be true to themselves and make the sport an expression of themselves. The sport and they act uniquely as one. As a master of your life, you create yourself as a unique, authentic expression of your purpose, gifts, talents, and virtues: your true authentic self, your soul. You are living your life in self-mastery.

Mastering your observer domain, which encompasses all aspects of your being, who you are, is the key to becoming the true architect of your life. It is in the knowing of being a spiritual being having a human experience that you live "from the inside out." Your soul, intuition, and imagination cause and direct your life. It is living and being a human being, not a human doing or having. Here, you understand the emotional domain and develop the courage to build a life beyond today's dreams. You develop the capacity and capability to behave and take actions that align with your deepest commitments. The journey of mastery leads to fulfilling your life vision, enabling you to be the architect of your future life, live with purpose, and experience a profoundly meaningful and fulfilling life.

Your commitment to mastering your observer domain will take your success to levels beyond your current dreams.

This is true success.

This is holistic success.

Let us dive deeper into our observer domain and explore three subdomains. I call these three domains the kaleidoscope of your observer. We live in these domains regardless of whether we are in our ego or soul observer. Yet *consciously* becoming aware of *how we use them* is a *rare and advanced skill.* They are also the bridge between the non-physical and your physical world. What is this kaleidoscope and bridges I am talking about? These are the domains of your body, emotions, and language.

Body – Emotions – Language

In life, a rare and advanced skill exists beyond the surface of our daily decisions and actions. Like the current in a river, unseen at the surface, yet powerfully guiding the river on its course. This rare and advanced skill is our ability to consciously create our life by knowing the transformative power that our body, emotions, and language hold. They function as the current in our lives, guiding us through life. But the commonly held belief by most people is that there is little or nothing to learn here because they already know and use them.

However, most people operate in a reactive mode with them. Given situations, circumstances, or what someone says or does, they react, acting out of habitual behaviors. Our body, emotions, and language express reactions and habitual behaviors.

The first step in understanding these domains is to become consciously aware of them and how they influence our lives. Then, to understand them, learning how much your body influences your quality of life, the messages and lessons emotions hold, and the power of your language catapults you on your journey to new levels of holistic success and self-mastery.

Please do not underestimate how critical it is to understand the phenomenon of their creative power and interconnectedness.

Let's begin by looking at how these domains act like kaleidoscopes in your life. We all have experienced a kaleidoscope and know that when you change the objects it is focused on, alter the lens, or both, you change the symmetrical patterns you see. This same principle applies when you alter any of these three domains. When you alter any of them, the other two align with the frequency of the first one. When you alter an emotion, for example, that emotion is expressed through your body and language.

For example, become angry (emotion) and watch your body constrict and your language express your anger. Conversely, have a romantic evening with your spouse/partner and see the changes in your body, emotions, and language!

To make your body, emotions, and language even more powerful, understand that they are also bridges. They are the bridge between your nonphysical and your physical reality. From the nonphysical aspect of our thoughts, feelings, senses, and beliefs, it is then through our body, emotions, and language that we shape and create our life. You use them to create and direct your life.

You use them to express who you are to the world.

But *the* fundamental question is, "Who is it expressing?"

- Ego Observer?
- Soul Observer?

You always have the power to choose.

Whether you are living your life from your egoic construct or the wisdom of your soul, you are constantly using these domains to shape, create, and live your life. The power of your transformation lies in knowing that if you are operating in your ego observer, you are all but guaranteed to react to things happening in your life. In higher consciousness, the soul observer, you *respond* into life being a creator being.

Let us look at each one of them to understand them better individually.

Body

The body is not just a physical entity but a way you engage with your environment. Remember, we are spiritual beings having a human experience. It is in our body that our soul has a human experience. Being in better physical condition means that the more vibrant our body is, the better experience we give to our soul.

It influences your energy levels, health, movement, and even how you communicate non-verbally. The physical state of your body can significantly impact your perspective and actions. When well-rested, nourished, and in good health, you are more likely to make sound decisions and be in a positive state of mind. Conversely, neglecting your physical well-being can lead to stress, anxiety, and impaired decision-making. Your physical well-being makes a difference in how you navigate through life, experience life, and show up in life. Your body also influences the level of inspiration you have to fulfill your life vision, live with purpose, and have a fulfilling life. If you do not have the physical strength to live the life you create for yourself, your life is compromised. This is another reason SOAR teaches holistic success, to not compromise your health for the sake of success in other areas of your life.

Here is an extraordinary example of the correlation between the body, emotions, and language. And sorry

I can't cite the source of this story, but I want to say it was either Joe Dispenza, Bruce Lipton, or Greg Bradon... at least I remember it was a reputable source. Anyway, a person has cancer. This person has a car accident, causing amnesia. Having amnesia, they forgot they had cancer, and their body healed itself of cancer. They forgot, no longer knowing, to talk about it. The power of language, your self-talk, and its effects on your body!

Emotions

Consciously understanding and managing your emotions and moods is a rare and advanced communication skill. Even rarer and more advanced is understanding that emotions come with a meaning and a message. Combined, this knowledge is life-altering!

Emotions, "Yes, so what, I have them." This is the general belief system of most of humanity, which can be called the culture. Since the Scientific Revolution, we have been taught to ignore, discard, suppress, invalidate, and try to control our emotions. If we allow them to express, we mostly *react* from the triggered emotion instead of creating and holding (now it becomes a mood) a higher-level emotion, and *responding into the circumstance that initially triggered our lower frequency emotion*. That is if we still want to deal with the issue. Raising our consciousness and emotions may cause us to transcend the issue and refocus on our future vision.

Understanding that you have emotions but are not your emotions and that you manage them, not control them, is the beginning of learning about them. Emotions also come with messages and lessons, messages and lessons that help you evolve, transform, and heal your life. But you must be open to hearing them to learn from them.

Also, knowing you manage your emotions allows you to create any emotion you want, regardless of what happens in your outer world. Few know this, and fewer do it. This is why mastering this domain is a rare and advanced skill in life.

Emotions and moods play a crucial role in shaping your observer's viewpoint. They shape and impact our thoughts, decisions, and behaviors. They shape our relationships, drive our motivations, and help us make sense of our experiences. Our emotional state determines how we interpret and respond to events in life. Yet, arguably, this domain is given the least attention of these three domains, the least time and energy to learn and understand it.

A few examples. Fear, anger, hate, craving, anxiety, regret, guilt, blame, shame, humiliation, and hopelessness are all low vibration emotions. All exist in the egoic construct. They all give the lens, the energy, the frequency, the consciousness, and the starting point, in which you engage with life and form your perspectives and perceptions of yourself, others, and the world. And low vibration emotions are very limiting and constricting. They shut down your thinking and openness to options, often engaging your sympathetic nervous system, fight, flight, or freeze. Alas, a law of the universe is always at your side: what you put out, you receive. Low energy emotions and the egoic construct can create and keep you in a life of hell. Conversely, raising your consciousness alters your emotions and mood into gratitude, joy, happiness, peace, compassion, forgiveness, and love. Your world expands, you change your perceptions and perspectives of yourself, others, and the world. And you completely alter the starting point from which you deal with anything or anyone in your life. You are now operating in your parasympathetic nervous system. Now you are more relaxed and open. This is how you create heaven on earth.

When you understand emotions and moods, you enter an advanced way of communicating and being that helps and supports you. Grounded in your soul observer, and acting as the creator you are designed to be, you can create a life of magic.

As your soul observer, you know you have emotions, but you are not your emotions. You observe the emotion as it comes up and choose whether to react when you are in the emotion. Especially if it is a low vibration emotion, it is likely best for you, and all concerned, not to react when you are in that emotion. Instead, breathe through the emotion and then consciously choose how, and in what emotion, you will *respond*. What emotion will you create for yourself... you are a divine creator! Compassion, understanding, gratitude, joy, and peace are some of the highest emotions we can operate in.

Emotions also come with a message. Mastery in one's life is being able to observe the emotion without reacting to it. To pause and look for the gifts and lessons they hold, and to then be open and curious to learn. Use them to learn the lesson the emotion or mood shares with you. This is a way in which you can break through your cognitive dissonance. This is how and where you open doors to a world of new knowledge and insights.

How important of a role your moods and emotions play in getting the results you want in your life. They are critical to your success. If you can feel it, you can do it. Because moods and emotions equate to degrees of willingness. As a divine creator, you have the ability to generate moods and emotions to help and support you in fulfilling your life vision and living your life with purpose and fulfillment. Do you see the secret to manifesting your holistic success here? You can always generate a mood of already having the success you want. You feel it, own it. Be in alignment with the result commitment, energetically, before you take a single action.

Emotions are also precursors to the actions we take. If you let your emotions control you or think you are your emotions, you will find yourself reacting to life. You will become like the little silver ball in the pinball game that gets batted around by the flippers. The little silver ball has no control over where it is going.

Thinking you are your emotion and reacting based on the emotion that got triggered causes you to not be in control of your life and lose focus on your life vision and purpose. You then travel to unseen and unplanned places the uncontrolled emotion sends you. This journey often comes with regret. And it always comes at a high cost: time, money, energy, and lost opportunity!

How can you begin to transform how you *manage* your emotions? We are so conditioned, operating in an unconscious manner, habitually, to react to every circumstance, situation, event, or person that arises or comes into our lives that pushes one of our buttons. We believe that reacting is normal, and it is what we should do, at the expense of being open to being aware that we *always* have a choice.

A choice to react or respond.

A choice in who is responding – ego or soul observer.

The moment you react to something, that is the moment you give your power over to what you reacted to.

What you resist persists.

And there is more. What you put out, you get back: the universal Laws of Cause and Effect and the Law of Attraction are, just like gravity, always at work. If you are reacting to circumstances, situations, events, and people that you say you don't like, don't want, cause you stress, anxiety, breakdowns, yet you are constantly reacting to them... the universe keeps giving you more of what you say you don't want!

Again, you are not your emotions; you have emotions. You do not control your emotions; you manage them. You always have the power to create and hold your emotions and moods with intention. You are the cause of your life; nothing or no one else is.

Here is another critical element to why you want to understand the sheer power of emotions. Emotions are energy, energy in motion. To quote Einstein, "Energy cannot be created or destroyed; it can only be changed from one form to another." When you suppress, repress, deny, or ignore your emotions, energy does not just vanish or go away. Stay on this path long enough, and it will manifest in the physical. It is called breakdowns, "accidents" (there are no accidents in life), and dis-ease.

If you are in the consciousness of ego, small self, and harboring those lower vibration emotions, it is but a matter of time before they will express themselves in the physical, your body.

There is another path.

Instead of reacting, especially when your lower vibration emotions are triggered, learn to stop, reflect, and learn. Reflect on which observer self you reacted from, the ego or the soul? A hint for you, a soul never reacts, it can only respond. What does the emotion triggered have to teach you? When you can raise your emotion to a high level, you can choose to respond or not, as the issue at hand may become a non-issue. You just transcended it.

In Viktor Frankl's famous quote, "Between the stimulus and response, there is a space. And in that space lies our freedom and power to choose our responses. In our response lies our growth and our freedom."

However, the critical question and distinction is, who are you as your observer choosing your response?

You as your ego?

You as your soul?

Your choice as your observer leads to you living in different worlds!

Here is another rare skill for your life. When any of the lower vibration emotions are tripped, you stop, breathe, and change the context of the emotion being tripped. See the circumstance, situation, event, or person as a *teacher!* See it or them as caring enough about you to trigger your emotion as an opportunity to heal your hurt. That lower vibration emotion would have never tripped unless something inside of you needed to be healed. Never. Heal the hurt, and then it will be impossible for the lower vibration emotions to be triggered. You will have healed and transcended what caused you to have the lower vibration emotion initially triggered. And if you have a breakdown with someone, with you both becoming upset, know you are both pounding on each other's buttons, showing each other what you each have to heal. Are you going to be the one to rise above the low-level emotions, to have courage, and take the high road? To raise your consciousness? To raise your energy? To be a way-shower to the other person, showing them how to heal, and act with respect and compassion in a state of higher consciousness?

You may want to act on the emotion initially triggered for a moment, but as you practice this learning, your reaction periods will shorten and eventually vanish. It will take you less and less time to shift into higher consciousness and raise your emotions when faced with a breakdown. You will see and experience it as an opportunity to be in and sustain higher energies and consciousness, to act from self-empowerment, and to be a way-shower!

Remember, the Law of Attraction and Cause and Effect are *always working!*

As a creator, a spiritual being, having a human experience, with free will, you are, in your essence, a high vibration energy being. To deny this is to not be true to your Self. To deny this is a function of self-destruction.

To consciously generate, hold, and manage your emotions at this level is a rare and advanced communication skill that perhaps 1% of the population knows and uses. Yes, it is that rare and powerful!

Knowing this rare and advanced communication skill gives you access to true self-empowerment, helping and supporting you on your transformational journey.

This is how you become the cause and creator of your life, *no matter what your current reality is.*

Language

We are both human beings and linguistic beings. We live in language.

People always communicate with each other; this is how we navigate through life. You communicate in many ways, not only with others but with yourself. Therefore, the commonly held belief is "I know how language works." Yet, when you learn this domain, it will be like walking around with a crystal ball as you can know a person's all but certain future just by the way they talk... but others simply cannot see this. The same thing applies to your life. When you consciously become aware of your self-talk, you will also know your all but certain future.

The way our world occurs to us occurs in language. It creates meaning and shapes our understanding of reality. It defines how we articulate our thoughts, frame experiences, and influence others. And all of this causes our inner dialogue, how we communicate with ourselves, and how we communicate with others. It is your communication that influences and shapes the actions you take and the results you achieve in life.

The results you achieve define your success. Clear, effective communication leads to better outcomes, while miscommunication or misunderstandings hinder your success and cause breakdowns.

Your language is the cause of either your *word creating your world* or your *world creating your word* (you may want to reread this sentence).

The Bible says, "In the beginning was the word..." Reflect on how powerful this is: you are a divine creator!

Why do we call it spelling? Because our words cast a spell... words - language - manifests your world.

Prayer is a form of casting a spell.

In fact, according to Dr. Leonardo Horowitz, "one-third of the sensory motor cortex of the brain is devoted to the tongue, oral cavity, the lips, and speech. In other words, oral frequency emissions spoken or sung exert powerful control over life, vibrating genes that influence total well-being and even the evolution of the species."

Regardless of which observer you are, we operate from two language domains: *descriptive or generative.* The sky is blue, which is a descriptive language; it describes. Please pass the salt as an example of generative language, as it generates action.

Descriptive Language

Is your life given by your language coming from a place of hopes, dreams, and wishes? As linguistic beings, we navigate life through the language we use. It is our language that shapes our experience of reality. And descriptive language that most people use to relate to their world. It reflects what it is, recounting past events, current circumstances, or future aspirations. Descriptive language is also the domain of playing it safe… very safe… in your life. Your ego loves this domain. It seeks agreement and validation here. It is one of its safety nests.

Descriptive language is, as the name implies, describes. Most people hang out almost full-time in this domain. The exception is obtaining their basic needs in life when they use generative language. They describe their world and others' world (a.k.a. gossip) and talk about hopes, dreams, and wishes. They describe their desires but remain passive observers of their lives, without actively shaping the outcomes. Descriptive language outlines the terrain but does not move the speaker toward any particular destination. While it may feel good to operate in your life in this domain, it is not the domain of being able to fulfill your results commitments!

Instead, it is the realm of "someday," "if only," and "I wish," where people reflect but seldom act. But you are on a path of holistic success, self-mastery, and

SOARing! And while descriptive language is useful and needed at times, it is our next domain of language that is where you primarily create your life from.

Generative Language

Language. "In the beginning was the word," which should be a major indication of how important language is to us. Science has now proven that we can recode our DNA through the use of our words. Yes, change our physical essence via the power of our words.

In our human experience, we live in language. Yet, despite its importance, we most often take language for granted. People often believe that they are proficient in language because they can talk, communicate with others, and use grammar (mostly) correctly. What we are not taught, what we are not aware of, is the ontological use of language. As human beings living in language, SOAR teaches you how to use language to *consciously* create your life.

We use language to accomplish things in our lives, and it touches every aspect of our lives. But we use it with little or no regard for its power. Generative language plays a crucial role in how we engage with others. In generative language lies our power to create our lives. We need to be able to take actions that are aligned with our purpose and life vision. All of us are using our language to create our lives today, whether conscious of this or not, so within, so without. Our lives are a reflection of our inner dialogue, without exception. Generative language is a major ingredient in causing your future life and holistic success.

Generative language, as the name implies, generates. It is the creative force of language. Here is an example of the transformative power it holds when you shift your language: "I can't do this," which limits action. Instead, "I am committed to finding a way through this challenge." This opens the doors to possibilities and solutions. This latter statement does not just describe the current situation. Instead, it sets the stage for new outcomes. It gives you a new starting point to deal with the issue. Feel the shift in your energy when you read these two statements. Generative language distinguishes and produces actions that produce your desired results. Language is energy. Generative language aligns you with having already fulfilled your results commitment before you take action. A major example of generative language is the U.S. Declaration of Independence. The founding fathers of the U.S. declared a new country into existence.

A declaration is the most powerful form of generative language you can use. As the name implies, you declare something into existence or to happen. When you are your soul observer, connected to your essence, and using generative language, your transformative power does not get any more powerful. We are divine creators made in the image and likeness of God. I am is the most powerful two words, declaration, you can speak. When God said to Moses, "I am that I am," that statement defines the power of I am. Using the famous and powerful words given to Moses is also the most powerful declaration you can declare for yourself, "I am that I am." Use this sentence as a declaration for your life, an affirmation, and a prayer. You are affirming your essence, your truth, and your divinity with this declaration. You are generating yourself as your true authentic self with this declaration.

The words you speak after "I am" complete the declaration. From declarations such as "I am stupid" to "I am a genius" and everything in between, you are declaring it to be so.

When you consciously become aware of your use of language, it initially appears as though you are a magician... especially regarding others. The power of generative language lies in its ability to create new futures. Listen to what people say as they are telling you about their almost certain future. Once you begin to see this in others, it is time to apply it to yourself.

Your spoken and self-talk words describe, define, and declare "it" to be so, generating your almost certain future. As your soul observer self, it is about creating new realities and expanding what you believe is possible by declaring them to be so... now. In the present, it is declaring your future into existence regardless of what your life is today.

What are you creating, divine creator?

People speak primarily from a reactionary and subconscious place, with little or no thought about what they say. They also use descriptive language far more often than generative language. Augmenting this is, as I have previously shared, humanity mostly lives in stories. But again, we forget they are stories, believing them to be the truth. If you use generative language in your stories, you generate more of the story. It is not right or wrong, good or bad, but rather about bringing awareness to how you use language and subsequently manifest things and people in your life.

Most people live past-focused lives based on their egos, living in stories created long ago. They believe these stories of the past to be the truth and mostly unconsciously use descriptive language to navigate this stew of life. And in this context, they are trying to be successful. This is the definition of traditional success: defined by your past and having it define you.

In contrast, declaring yourself to be your soul observer causes you to transcend in consciousness, seeing beyond your limitations, and begin to take actions aligned with your purpose and declared result. This is creating your life and your future, being connected to your heart's wisdom, and guided by your intuition and imagination. This is also being true to your higher self. This is also how you live an inspired (in-spirit) life instead of being motivated by the material world. Whether you are making a promise, asking for support, or declaring a new vision, generative language shifts you from being a passive observer of your life to an active creator. By understanding and using generative language, you can transform habitual patterns, break old limiting beliefs, reshape relationships, and open yourself to the infinite potential of life's unfolding possibilities.

You must use language in anything you want to do, create, or have. To be successful, as you define success, requires using generative language. The fulfillment of your results commitments requires you to coordinate actions with both you and others, which aligns with accomplishing your results. It is generative language that you primarily use to create and define the necessary actions you need to take.

"Who is going to do what by when?" is an enormously powerful use of generative language. You are generating something to happen by a specific date and/or time. Do not let the simplicity of this sentence elude you from thinking it is not powerful. I have used this sentence on more than one occasion. One example of how powerful this question is. I was very challenged to get the results I wanted for a project I was involved in. Results that both the other party and I agreed to. But it wasn't happening. I asked the "who is going to do what by when" question, and initially, they did not understand it. No one had ever asked them that question. I did get my result.

Most breakdowns happen because of one of two reasons inside this sentence: "Who is going to do what by when?" First, there is a lack of clarity in understanding the desired outcome, the mutually agreed upon result commitment. The second, and larger, element of the cause of breakdowns is the by-when factor. Declaring a specific date and/or time when what will happen is often assumed, ambiguous, or completely left out of the conversation.

Generative language plays a critical role in fulfilling your results commitments when you are working with others, whether one individual or a team. Generative language also plays a crucial role in the conditions of satisfaction of the result commitment. Conditions of satisfaction define what needs to occur for all parties involved to fulfill the result commitment. You align actions primarily through generative language to fulfill your desired results. A simple, multi-gazillion-dollar (okay, maybe a little stretch here) example of conditions of satisfaction for you is Starbucks. Most of us have had a drink from Starbucks. They grab a paper or plastic cup, a hot or cold beverage, in the given size you ordered, and boxes are on the side of the cups. They check the boxes to reflect the conditions of satisfaction for your drink, the specific ingredients of the drink you ordered. You pay for the cup of coffee before receiving it, trusting that they will fulfill the conditions of satisfaction for your drink.

Do not overthink the conditions of satisfaction. They can be quite simple as well as extraordinarily complex. But without them, the chances of breakdowns significantly increase. In fact, a breakdown is all but guaranteed.

Knowing the power of language, you can see how it influences your life. How you create what you want in your life happens in language. How the world occurs to you, again, lives in language.

Remember, language also alters your emotions and body! This kaleidoscope always shows you and aligns with what you are focused on.

Defining your success and then having the results you get correlated to what you call success also occurs in language. But who is showing up, who are you, that is having conversations? Conversations with yourself and with others are needed to get the outcomes you want in your life.

Check back into your observer. *Are your words creating your world, or is your world giving your words?* Generative language is how your words create your world! Is it your ego observer or soul observer that is generating your language?

If you are going to know yourself as your soul observer, it initially takes courage to move from descriptive to generative language and to be in action.

Your language must be one of the leading factors that cause a transformative shift in your life. This applies to both the language you speak and your self-talk.

From having the desire to take action, language is most often our starting point and point of reference for the actions we take. Descriptive language is the domain of "I hope," "that would be nice," and language that lacks action. Conversely, generative language causes actions. "I am committed to making that happen," I am committed to finding a way through this challenge," calls you to be in action. Action to make your life better.

You become your word when you shift your observer self from ego to soul. Your word gives, creates, your world... divine creator. Be true to yourself! You also create actions that align with your virtues and what you care about most in your life. These lead to the results you are committed to, to the fulfillment of your results commitments.

What results are you promising yourself and others? Remember, the fulfillment and accomplishment of your results equals your success.

Can you see yourself as your word and virtues, and fulfill what you care about most? Can you see the difference in the results you achieve and your success? Are you in this domain instead of hanging out in the wants, feelings, and opinions domain? Yet another example of two different worlds. Two completely different contexts to come from to create your life. They both result in two distinct levels of success. More accurately, one gives you no success, and the other is the foundation of obtaining any level of success you desire.

When your language occurs in your virtues, what you care about most, honoring your promises, aligns with fulfilling your life vision, this is the land of risk and self-empowerment. This is the land of being extraordinary in your life!

Language, whether as thoughts, conscious self-talk, or overt conversations with others, never dismiss the power of language.

With your understanding of descriptive and generative language, you understand the profound impact that our linguistic choices have on shaping our lives. Generative language has the capacity to create new possibilities, opportunities, and realities. It has the power to transcend our past experiences, challenges, and struggles, with you emerging into a space of pure potential and transformation.

Continuing your journey of evolving, let's see how science has caught up to what the sages and mystics have known for eons. Again, the power of your word and how you can use it to create and embody your holistic success.

Recode Your DNA

Your self-talk creates your life, whether you are conscious of this or not. Things happen in life, and when they do, we give them meaning, also known as creating a story. Most of us do this unconsciously, habitually, given by our cultural and historical narratives, and with no awareness that we are doing it. You are living the life you are today, given by what you have been telling yourself with little or no regard for critically thinking about it.

With SOAR, this is your opportunity to *consciously create your future*, as you have been learning. But now imagine the exponential power of creating your future when you recode your DNA to align with the future you create. To "rewire" yourself for your holistic success.

You can recode your DNA with the power of your words! You can "rewire" your very essence and create a new future for yourself... regardless of your past!

Again, the sages and mystics have known this for eons, and scientists have recently proven it. This is being able to have your DNA transcend past limitations, problems, challenges, and struggles, and deepening your connection to your inner world. Having your inner world fully support you transforms your reality into your future holistically successful you.

There is a recipe for recoding your DNA. It takes time and perseverance, but the rewards far outweigh the efforts required.

Before I share this recipe to recode your DNA, I highly suggest you apply this recipe to your life vision. You author your life vision in six domains of your life, defining the results you are committed to in order to obtain your desired success. With SOAR, it is now your holistic success. Your life vision is steeped in the generative language to empower you to fulfill your results commitments. In short, your life vision serves as your personalized blueprint for your perfect future. There simply is nothing more powerful, clearer, or well-defined for you to recode your DNA to.

And I say "recode" your DNA, because we all have spent our entire lives encoding our DNA with our unconscious self-talk. This, at the level of your very essence, breaks the "wiring" of your past limitations, problems, and challenges. Now you create new neural pathways in your brain. Now you consciously encode your DNA with your future life. A future life that you have authored!

Okay... here is your recipe to recode your DNA.

1. Continue learning SOAR. Take on learning SOAR to mastery level. SOAR is your transformational blueprint for your life. It is a fundamental foundation with a multidisciplinary

and holistic approach to doing and having anything you want in your life. You can enjoy more holistic success by utilizing the strategies and tactics SOAR offers and raising your consciousness. The results of doing this give you more possibilities in higher consciousness to recode into your DNA.

2. Create your *Life Vision to Mastery*. This is your Self-created blueprint for your success! Your blueprint is created and designed connected to your soul, intuition, and imagination. It is also built on the philosophies of Ontology and Metaphysics. This is your personalized, multidisciplinary, and holistic approach to creating and designing... always and in the present... your ideal future life. It is the best, most accurate, and built on a framework of generative language, document to recode your DNA to.

3. Now, 6 times a day, you are going to read aloud, with passion and feeling, own it, in the present, as your current reality… because it is… your life vision to yourself for 21 days. 21 days is what it takes to *begin* to recode your DNA. 90 days is recommended to make lasting and profound changes to your life.

I invite you to reflect on this lesson and what you have learned with SOAR.

- Reflect specifically on the *Add POWER to Your Success section,* beginning on page 43.

- Reflect on the power of using generative language.

- Reflect on any additional new knowledge that stands out to you in the teachings of SOAR.

- Reflect on the insights you have gained in your new learning.

This is an excellent time to journal and capture your insights.

Tapped into your intuition and imagination, keep journaling. What do they want to tell you?

Are you beginning to *feel* the power you are harnessing to transform and transcend in your life and to create anything you desire?

An offer for you to radically transform your life, I offer a 30-day program combining SOAR and Life Vision to Mastery. See the Next Steps section at the end of the book for more information.

Remember, life is about our continuous evolution, your evolution to self-mastery. Recoding your DNA is your departure ticket from a reactive life. Instead, you embody being an active participant in creating your future.

Understanding the transformative power of your body, emotions, and language is a rare and advanced self-awareness skill. But in closing this section of SOAR, I want to cover two more distinctions: cognitive dissonance and courage. They both play essential roles in living a life of holistic success.

Cognitive Dissonance

Cognitive Dissonance often lives as a silent enemy to your success. It acts without your awareness of its existence. It comes in and takes control, limiting, hampering, or flat out preventing you from altering your life and to be able to obtain success. It happens mostly unconsciously and simply stated, keeps you in your lack and limitations. It also acts as a frequent enemy to your learning. Your cognitive dissonance has you holding on to your commonly held beliefs and locked in your limiting habits. In doing so, you are not open to your divine wisdom.

Cognitive dissonance can limit and stop your success, and you can't see it. Initially, it is your thoughts and beliefs that cause your cognitive dissonance. Your body, emotions, and language reflect those thoughts and beliefs. But where do thoughts and beliefs almost always come from?

Your past!

Cognitive dissonance can lead a person to ignore or be unable to see other possibilities and opportunities. When presented with new possibilities and opportunities, instead of being open, we feel discomfort. Individuals often unconsciously filter out information that conflicts with their beliefs or choices to reduce or eliminate this discomfort. This selective perception allows them to maintain a sense of consistency in their thoughts and actions. It is not until the pain of life is greater than the pain of change that you break the shell of your cognitive dissonance.

Here is a real-life story as an example of what I believe is the power of a person's cognitive dissonance. The highly successful business development coach in this story is a friend of mine and shared this story with me. This story is about a salesperson who was struggling in his profession. And his struggle had been going on for a few years. He could not get above a certain level in his sales results, limiting his income. The struggling salesperson was given an opportunity to have lunch with my coach friend. A mutual friend set up a meeting for the three of them to have lunch together. The mutual friend in this story is also highly successful in his profession. He attributes his success to working with the coach for many years. The struggling salesperson knew in advance of their luncheon meeting about the long-term relationship between the salesperson and the coach. Now the three of them are having lunch together. It was assumed that the struggling salesperson would have a conversation about engaging with the coach. After all, the struggling salesperson knew his friend's success very well and what the coach could offer.

Lunch happened. No conversation occurred about the struggling salesperson working with the coach. None. I assume that the struggling salesman's cognitive dissonance was so strong that he could not discuss how his life could be different.

This story was shocking and sad to me. A fantastic opportunity is offered to a person who cannot go there. I know this story too well from my past personal struggles. Reflect on how often you may have been presented with an opportunity to transform it, to choose a "higher road" path, or a professional opportunity, and you could not see it then. Or your saboteur self managed to do something to thwart the opportunity. The power of our ego is staggering, especially when it is unconsciously in control. Our egos will defend, justify, validate, create stories, and seek agreement to keep us locked in our small selves. This is why it is essential to be hyperaware of our body, emotions, and language. They are the keys to our transformation. Our thoughts, beliefs, feelings, and habits are expressed through them.

Being ever mindful of who you are operating as in your life: ego observer or soul observer. This determines how you create and manage your body, emotions, and language. Operating in your ego observer, it is doubtful that you will see your cognitive dissonance. You will believe what you are seeing or experiencing as the truth.

Transforming your cognitive dissonance happens when you are your soul observer. This is when you are open to new and different ideas and perceptions, when your old habit patterns tell you not to be. The exercises of journaling and reflection give you insights into your cognitive dissonance. Transforming your cognitive dissonance will help your relationships with persistence and determination. To better manage them, know if or when to turn them up or off. And when to *stay open and not be attached to the outcome.* Having the awareness of how your cognitive dissonance may be preventing your success is a lesson unto itself. But beginning to know about it and seeing ways it hinders your success is the first step in transforming it.

Transforming and transcending your cognitive dissonance takes courage and faith. But whatever it takes to overcome its limitations, the benefits are beyond measure.

Courage

It takes courage to transform one's life, stepping outside of one's comfort zone and societal and cultural norms, and to be authentic. It often takes a lot of emotional courage to "be different" and honor oneself, despite what one's family and friends, culture, and even the world are showing you at the time.

The emotional domain is where and how you find the courage to embark on your journey of self-awareness, self-growth, personal transformation, and success. This is your continual journey to Self-realization.

The emotional domain is rich beyond measure. Only in the last few decades has humanity started to understand the importance of EQ, emotional Intelligence, in our lives. Learning the emotional domain is indeed a rare and advanced skill that has immeasurable benefits.

Let me offer a few examples of the power of understanding your emotions and their transformative power in your life.

Anger. An extremely popular emotion in today's world. Someone says something or does something, and you become angry. You feel angry because you feel there was an injustice to you in what was said or done. A perceived injustice causes anger; by extension, anger can point to justice. I say perceived, because in the initial reaction phase of feeling anger, your story about what happened is causing your anger. This is another reason not to react but to seek understanding from the other person or people before acting. It is always best to never react but instead to respond. And here is why. When you let anger control you, you react; your body, emotions, and language align with the energy of anger, and this is what happens.

When we drop into anger, and I say "drop" because you just hit the down button on your mood elevator and went to a low vibration emotion. Anger takes our body into the fight, flight, or freeze mode. It tightens up like a brick, the physiology of our body changes. We are no longer open to thinking clearly. Instead, we are entirely focused on our perceived injustice. We are no longer open, period. Our breathing becomes shallow and fast, just the opposite of getting ourselves into higher states of consciousness when we breathe slowly and deeply. And our language reflects our belief in injustice, often blaming or punishing the person we perceive as doing us an injustice. Most often, and especially if our anger has digressed to rage, the words that come out of our mouth are extremely low vibration and we are "vomiting" our anger. Think about how constricted your heart is in this emotion!

In fact, the term heart attack is entirely wrong. Our heart never attacks us! Instead, living for extended periods of time with our heart chakra closed, ignoring or completely not being conscious of and connected to our heart's wisdom, causes heart dis-ease.

Remember, we are designed for our heart's wisdom to be the master, our brain to be the servant, and our intuition to be our guiding voice. For God knows how long, we have been living in complete opposition to how we are designed and how our essence is structured.

In contrast, how would it be different if we increased our courage? In the emotion of courage, we address our initially perceived injustice and discover the whole story and the real issue. And from courage, understanding, and knowing the whole story, we respond to the other person with compassion.

Compassion is one of the highest emotions we can be in. It is when our heart's wisdom and our "head," our brains, work together. But our heart's wisdom is always primary.

Compassion does not mean you must agree with injustice if there truly is one. Nor does it mean you have to continue to work or associate with the person. But compassion causes you to be open. Openness allows you to deal with injustice in a completely different context than the emotion of anger.

Let me give you another example of our mood elevator on the opposite side of this spectrum. Let's hit our mood button and go from the low energy of anger and raise our emotion to gratitude. Feel the difference in your energy, your openness, and the shift in your body and language as they align to the change in your emotional state.

And let us begin in the same space as the example of anger. Someone says something or does something, and you become angry. You feel angry because you feel that there is an injustice to you in what was said or done. You initially want to react with your anger, but this time you hit your pause button and breathe.

Just be for a moment. Just be for as long as it takes to let the feeling of anger run its course. I love the metaphor of seeing your anger as a cloud in the sky. Observe it, do not react, and let it pass by.

And now what?

You're a divine creator, you're powerful. Create your emotion to be in gratitude. And you are thinking, "Someone just screwed me over, or tried to, and you want me to be grateful!?!" Yes! First, I am not saying to deal with the perceived injustice that caused your anger. I am saying anchor yourself in a higher emotion and allow your body and language to align with this higher emotion first.

Second, here is the critical distinction. Take the high road. Gratitude is a very high-vibration emotion. Consciously creating and holding this emotion when dealing with the person or people involved in the issue, and why your anger button was tripped, is a rare and advanced communication skill! Very rare!

Next, acknowledge yourself. You stopped, breathed, and courageously changed course on this issue. On the high road, with courage at your side, let's look at how responding in gratitude to a perceived injustice is compared to reacting in anger.

Again, the physiology of our body changes. Now, you are open, calm, and able to think clearly. You remain focused on the perceived injustice and can listen to the other person and seek to understand them. Being open and calm, you can clearly assess why you reacted angrily. Your breathing stays slow and deep, allowing you to sustain a higher mood of gratitude. Your language reflects your belief in injustice, but in a completely different context than the emotion of anger.

Note: the only difference between an emotion and a mood is the time in which we experience it. An emotion is short-term, while moods are held over a longer time. The mastery of this communication skill, and another reason it is a rare and advanced skill, is that few people can maintain their emotions long enough to become moods when dealing with an issue such as this example.

Instead of ripping into someone, blaming, or punishing them, you seek to understand them and hold the space as an example of being able to have a respectful conversation when an injustice has occurred. Operating in gratitude with your body and language aligned, you are centered in your power. You come from a place of true self-empowerment to deal with the perceived injustice. Whether the injustice was real, intentional, or not, becomes secondary. Primary is who you become to resolve it.

I invite you to pause.

Breathe.

Can you feel the difference in dealing with an injustice in a higher-level emotion?

So, the perceived injustice. Managing it with gratitude, we have one of two endings to the story. First, we come to understand that what happened was not intentional. There was a breakdown because of a lack of communication. Because you are operating in gratitude, you have paved the path of being able to have a conversation with respect on "the high road," and the chances of coming to a mutually satisfactory resolution are remarkably high. You also gain trust and respect because you were the way-shower in managing the breakdown. You were an example of how to be calm, respectful, and self-empowered. In contrast, reacting in anger is just the opposite in all aspects.

The second ending to the story is that you find out that the person intentionally did an injustice to you. They showed their true character to you. Uncovering this makes it easier to fall into anger. But stay with gratitude, with the other person showing you their values and character. Be grateful that you can complete the relationship immediately, and hopefully, before too much injustice is done. Being resolute, combined with your higher consciousness emotion, is an advanced way to resolve the issue, which would be your next best step if the injustice was intentional.

If deliberate injustice was done, maintaining gratitude or any other applicable high-consciousness emotion keeps you relaxed and calm, allowing you to think clearly. Can you see the significant advantages you have in resolving this compared to someone locked in the emotion of anger?

Again, ego observer or soul observer. You always have the power of choice. And yes, facing your fears and unconscious habits takes courage. But what is it costing you not to face them? As your soul observer, you have the courage to step into your self-empowerment.

It isn't magic. It is acquiring new knowledge, which gives you access to new insights and new possibilities.

New knowledge.

New insights.

New possibilities.

New actions.

New results.

New levels of success.

Now you are SOARing!

Never underestimate the power of your body, emotions, and language, individually and collectively. Your emotions are precursors to your actions, which give you the results you get in life. The fulfillment of your results commitments that you define gives you your success.

How are you doing with embodying the SOAR model?

Can you see things open for you?

I am offering you an opportunity to pause and reflect on this section. The following are reflective questions to deepen your awareness of the kaleidoscope between your body, emotions, and language and their role as bridges between your nonphysical and physical realities. These questions also explore cognitive dissonance, success, and the courage required to transform your life.

Here are some reflection questions to help you embody this learning. Let's begin with your body awareness:

- What physical sensations do you notice when you feel aligned to one of your results commitments versus when you feel resistance, out of alignment, or stuck trying to accomplish them?

- How does your posture, breathing, and facial expression change when you alter your emotional state?

- How do your emotions and thoughts respond when you consciously relax a tense part of your body?

- How often do you pause and check in with your body during moments of stress, fear, or excitement?

- How does your body function as a messenger between your inner world, thoughts, emotions, and outer actions?

- What physical practices (e.g., movement, breathwork, stretching) help you to bridge the gap between your spiritual insights and physical experiences?

- Can you *f-e-e-l* where you are stuck in your life? Think of an area you feel stuck in and scan your body for where you feel tightness.

Your body is constantly communicating with you.

Emotional awareness:

- What emotions do you most often experience? How are they shaping your physical state and your language?

- Notice any emotions you are suppressing or ignoring and their effect on your body and the words you choose.

- What happens when you intentionally shift your emotional state, choosing compassion over anger, for example?

- How do your emotions influence the way you express yourself and the way you hold your body?

- How are your emotions connecting your nonphysical intentions, your intentions and purpose, to your physical actions and results commitments?

- What emotions do you consciously need to bring into your life to support and align you with your holistically successful life?

Language awareness:

- What words or phrases do you habitually use that reflect your current reality, and how do they compare, or what words would you use to reflect your evolving, successful self?

- How do your words influence your emotions and physical state? For example, the difference between "This is hard" and "This is a great opportunity to learn."

- When you describe challenges in your life, do you use language of limitation or possibilities?

- How can you use affirmations and intentional speech to align your body and emotions with your future vision?

- What new ways of speaking or framing a situation could bridge the gap between your spiritual insight and physical experience?

Kaleidoscope reflection questions

- When you change one aspect, body, emotion, or language, how do the other two naturally follow?

- Which of the three is easiest for you to shift, and which one feels the most challenging?

- How can you consciously create more harmony between your body, emotions, and language during times of stress, doubt, and fear?

- What small daily practice would help you to align your body, emotions, and language?

Cognitive dissonance reflection questions

- Where in your life are you saying one thing but feeling or doing something else?

- How does this internal misalignment appear in your physical sensations, emotions, or language patterns?

- In what ways has cognitive dissonance prevented you from accomplishing the success you say you want in your life?

- What belief, assumption, or story is at the root of your cognitive dissonance?

- How can you reframe or rewrite the story holding you back?

- How can you align your thoughts, emotions, body, language, and actions with your true authentic self?

Courage and faith reflection questions

- What is one area of your life that you feel you are being called to step into the unknown, but fear is holding you back?

- How can you build trust in yourself and the process, even if your reality suggests otherwise?

- Have you taken a leap of faith before, and what was the outcome?

- How does having faith feel in your body and emotions, and what language supports your faith?

- What one action can you take to align with your future vision?

- What does your future self, who already has the success and accomplishments you seek, want to tell you?

- What does your intuition tell you?

- What is your imagination showing you?

Summation reflection questions

- Are you having success in one area of your life and suffering in other areas of your life?

- Are new possibilities and new perspectives showing up for you?

- Are you aware of being able to consciously choose a new starting point when you address a problem or challenge from your past?

- Where are you emotionally? Are you feeling low-level, heavy emotions? If so, take a couple of deep breaths, change your language, move your body, and cause yourself to be in a higher-frequency emotion, such as compassion or gratitude.

- Is your success in the traditional or holistic domain?

- How can you use your body, emotions, and language as tools to dissolve your cognitive dissonance, embrace courage, and fully step into your soul observer to create anything you want for your life?

Learning to manage your body, emotions, and language to create and design your life transforms it. By understanding their interconnectedness and power, you now understand how to consciously use them to create, design, and live your life with purpose and fulfillment.

They are the drivers for you to live your unlocked potential!

This is the power of SOAR being experiential; you must live it to experience its benefits. Remember, awareness is the starting point of all transformation. Becoming aware of these three domains, how interlaced they are, and how they create your life is your first step to harnessing their power. Most of us go through life unconsciously aware of how we manage and use our bodies, emotions, and language. We think we have and use them, which qualifies us as proficient and knowledgeable in their use. But this is not true.

When you become conscious of how you unconsciously use something, this opens you up to new knowledge. New knowledge also opens you to new insights. With new knowledge and new insights, you have access to new choices. Choices that, but a moment ago, you didn't know existed. New choices very often give new starting points to issues. And from a new starting point, you engage with a new vision and new capacities. Now you are causing new levels of success in your life, holistic success.

Success

Success is a multifaceted concept that often eludes clear definition.

The question regarding your success is, "*What* defines your success?" But the defining and transformative distinction for your success is to change the question to "*Who* defines your success?"

This now gives us two domains of success: traditional success, which is how most of the world defines success, and holistic success. Holistic success is living your life inside out, where your divine wisdom not only creates what you author as your success but also does it in all areas of your life to live a harmonious life. Let's first look at what we call traditional success.

Is your success given by your egoic construct, separation, competition, winning at all costs, a mindset of "he/she who has the most toys wins"? Of having and doing any one, or more, of the countless variables, things, "shiny new objects" in the material world? Are you striving to keep up with someone or measuring yourself against someone else? Perhaps your shadow (Carl Jung) is in control of your life? Or do you feel a void in your life that is in control of defining your success? You work toward filling a void, thinking that the fulfillment of it would cause your success.

We strive to satisfy our shadows and fill our voids without thinking about why we do. We unconsciously live our lives this way, believing that the fulfillment of what we are chasing will give us success. Most often, nothing could be further from the truth. You can tell if you are working in this domain because you are primarily process-focused and focused on what you will do to be successful.

Also, most of our definitions of success are given and defined by our history and culture. Our history and culture are indelibly part of our lives. Today's marketing profession amplifies this, and we spend bazillions of dollars buying what they are marketing. They employ psychologists to exploit "I'm not good enough" and weave that into our history and cultural stories to sell us the craziest things imaginable.

Marketing also idolizes people with the biggest and newest "shiny new objects." Look at what professional sports figures and top actors get paid. This reflects what the mass consciousness of humanity values in life. And those who do not have those shiny new objects are too often made to feel less than. In fact, in the U.S., we have a crisis of "I'm not worth it." We have been taught to think that if we could ever get "one of those" or be like that person, we will also be successful. This is a grand illusion; nothing could be further from the truth. This belief system pulls us further from the truth of who we are!

But this is all a culmination of our history, culture, the material world, our past, and is ego-based. It is a massive house of cards. There is no space, awareness, or consciousness for things to be different on this ride.

It is striving for success without thinking about why we do it. Our cultural narratives almost exclusively define and control us from our *unconscious self*. They play huge roles, if not exclusively, in defining what constitutes our success. Our *unconscious beliefs* define us, and we believe them to be normal and *The Truth*.

Careers also have a way of defining your success, and defining you, period. How successful we are in our careers and how much money we make primarily defines this type of success. The never-ending chase for power, fame, and wealth.

Professional success is further defined by who you associate with, your accomplishments, and your achievements. So much so that many people have their careers at the center of their lives, and everything else fits in or works around them. Again, the never-ending chase for power, fame, and wealth defines us. This type of success puts the essence of who you are, your connection to your heart's wisdom, and your spiritual and personal life, at best, in second place. Most likely, little or no thought is given to these two domains. Other areas of your life suffer as well.

One's physical well-being and relationships also take a seat in the back of the bus... or get tossed off the bus.

And life beyond, in time, your professional life, retirement, or transitioning out of your full-time profession. Retirement comes with a lot of stories given by our history and culture. These stories are very diverse yet share a common element, made up of common stories and themes, where life lacks true purpose and fulfillment. Many people devote their lives to their professions only to get "right-sized" out of a profession, be laid off, or face health issues, causing them to have to stop working, or come to the time to retire. These paths often lead to the same end: a life with no purpose, meaning, or plan for tomorrow. You can only play golf, travel, or lie on the beach for so long, and for most of us, there comes a time when you feel something is missing in life.

Here is another aspect of success. This is especially relevant since we live in such a high-tech world. In the traditional definition of success, a successful person would be the "technocrat." Technocratic people live and define themselves according to the domain of results. To the extreme of this, this person does not care about how the results are accomplished; they just want the results. This world of technocrats lacks soul. They work in silos; the niche aspect of the IT profession serves as an excellent example. The person specializes in one element of the massive

114

technological world, where they operate to fulfill the tasks required to keep the system up and running. Let me share a story of a person I know as an example of how this may out picture and how it is void of soul.

He is a successful IT professional, having worked in the profession for decades. Today, he is diabetic. Diabetes, in part, means the person needs to control life, and that there is no sweetness in life (*You Can Heal Your Life*, Louise Hay). Do you see the connection between the IT world and diabetes? A person controls what and how they control their life and things in their life, and they're working to control what their industry does.

The industry's collective energy is continually working to control how they can do more, do it faster, and do it better while controlling the system. Where is the sweetness in that? There isn't. Diabetes is another example of how dis-ease manifests in the body when someone only knows being task-driven, traditional success, and success that lacks soul.

Here is another example of the horrific price traditional success can have on individuals. Based on *A Course in Miracles,* we are only capable of two emotions: fear and love. The U.S. military-industrial complex is the largest fear-based enterprise the world has ever experienced. This is the pinnacle of traditional success. The cost of this success? In 2020, the latest statistics Google gave me, "the age and sex adjusted suicide rate among Veterans was 57.3% higher than the age and sex adjusted rate among non-Veteran U.S. adults." There is absolutely no soul in the traditional success model of the military. The numbers sadly speak for themselves.

Working in the senior market in the mortgage profession for several years, I have often witnessed the breakdowns people experience in their retirement, or golden years, which are not so golden, because of a lack of planning and purpose. Additionally, they lack the awareness that they don't have to live their stories of lack, limitation, hardship, unhappiness, and a lack of purpose that so many of our stories born in our history and promoted throughout our cultures teach us.

With most people defining their success by what they do and have, there are good reasons for this to be this way. From day one, this is what we are taught. We are born into a society, a culture, with traditions, often a religion, all steeped in stories from our history. Stories we often live the rest of our lives having them define us, and we justify and defend ourselves with little or no understanding of why we do this! We accept this as the truth without consciously becoming aware of why this is so! Our history and culture are taken as the truth with little or no thought given as to why they are the way they are.

The truth about history and culture is that they focus on our past and outer world. All our stories are stories of what happened that someone gave meaning to. Whether you gave meaning to something that happened yesterday, or it is a story handed down for generations, it doesn't matter; it is a story from your past, and most likely, it plays its part in unconsciously controlling your life.

You may want to read this paragraph a few times, as this is the fundamental aspect of all our lives... until it is not. And I am not making or judging stories wrong; this is also a fundamental aspect of being human. But I am bringing awareness to how we all do it and how they *unconsciously* control our lives. It is our past-based stories that define success for most people. Bringing this awareness to you, and in doing so, we begin to disassemble the traditional definition of success. This is a significant and critical element of transforming your success.

In the last eighty years, and counting, there has been a radical shift in what constitutes our success. Since WWII, the marketing profession has told us that our lives will be better, fuller, and richer only if we have what they offer. We will be "somebody," we will be successful, we will have arrived. "They" encourage us to be like "them," and only then will our lives be good. Who are the "they and them?" It is a facade.

Everything in the material world is temporal.

The only constant is change. Yet, according to marketing gurus, buying what they offer, the "shiny new object," will make you a better person and make you successful.

In fact, they want you to think it will define your success.

This path of chasing shiny new objects is one of hollowness and emptiness. This path is giving your power over to the outside world. The ever-changing, temporal, fastest-changing, fastest-paced, most uncertain, material world comprised of stories from your past, outside world.

Remember, history, culture, traditions, and ego are all past-focused. This is where they justify their existence, defend their positions and beliefs, and seek agreement to validate their ways. Again, see a carousel here?! The only thing changing is the seat one rides in, but it is the same carousel.

Your history and culture are also where your problems and challenges are born. And if you constantly relive your past, you are continually reliving your problems and challenges. You are living a life with a self-imposed glass ceiling on your success in all areas.

I'm not saying throw out your history and culture, not at all. But I am offering that you consciously bring awareness to them and how they fit, or do not, into

118

your holistically successful life that you are about to create.

As you are about to learn with holistic success, you can bring as much of your history and culture into your life as you want. But now you are consciously doing it instead of having them unconsciously control your life. And whatever pieces of your history and culture you bring into your life, they support your success.

Traditional success is given and defined by our history, cultural narratives, and material world. Couple this with the psychological seduction of marketing, and it is no wonder you do not think about what constitutes your success. "They" are doing it for you!

Your inner world *is always* creating your outer world. However, most people lack this awareness and knowledge.

To transform your life, you need to redefine success. You need to define and then create your success from your inner wisdom. You need to go from "what" is creating your success to "who" is creating your success. Now, you are *consciously creating* your physical reality, your success. This is the difference between traditional and holistic success.

Holistic Success

People strive, often for a lifetime, to attain levels of success given by their history and culture. It may not be until this journey simply wears you out and causes a physical and/or emotional breakdown that you listen to what your inner wisdom has been trying to tell you.

Trying to have new success with the same level of consciousness and with the same knowledge, no new insights, simply put, is a recipe for failure. This is the traditional success model. Said differently, you say you want new levels of success, to improve your life, but you want to do it with the same level of knowledge, skills, and *consciousness.* How is that working out for you? There is a definition of insanity that fits here.

Despite your outward appearance of success, do you feel a hollowness within? Do you feel something is missing or something does not feel right? Do you have thoughts like "Is this all there is?" Or once you have achieved "that level of success," are you met with an internal void, a feeling of unfulfillment?

None of this is right or wrong.

Instead, it is about bringing awareness to your life.

Awareness gives you the power of choice.

120

Nothing happens without being aware of it. But awareness of something is meaningless in and of itself. The question is, once you gain awareness, do you have a desire to act? You can be aware of something but have no desire to act, no desire to change what you became aware of. You accept what is as it is. But if you desire to take action to change something given by your new awareness, your transformational power begins to unfold with your next step.

Your next step is not figuring out, "What am I going to do?" It is not about jumping into action. Instead, it is going within and looking to see what changes you can make in yourself. Where and how are you energetically out of alignment with your desired results? This is an internal journey of raising your consciousness, leading to self-transformation and transcendence, and gaining new insights.

This is your *river of gold.* These are the keys that unlock the gates, the keys to the kingdom. This is how you create new levels of holistic success in your life!

Gaining new insights is an internal journey. Insights give you sudden and profound realizations that transform understanding and perspectives. They happen outside of time. For example, you are walking down the grocery aisle looking at apples and you experience an epiphany about an issue you have been stressing over, the answer you have been searching for "drops in." They are personal and dynamic, happening in the space of who you are, your beingness. They are the fundamental drivers to transforming your life because they cause you to raise your consciousness. Higher consciousness causes you to seek new knowledge. Acting together, knowledge and insights cause you to redefine your success and subsequent result commitments and to take new and different actions. Actions that you previously could not see. Actions that you previously didn't have the capability or capacity to take.

On your SOARing journey, you will also acquire new knowledge. Knowledge is the accumulation of information, facts, and skills from our physical reality. You gain new knowledge through education, experience, or reasoning. A critical distinction about knowledge is that it exists regardless of whether you are aware of it or not. Moreover, gaining new knowledge almost never alters your consciousness. This sentence was radical to me when I discovered it. Knowing this helps you to understand yourself and others and why we do what we do. A couple of examples for you here. A brilliant person creates weapons of mass destruction, a reflection of their low level of consciousness. A brilliant person creates holistic healing devices, a reflection of their high level of consciousness. Knowledge exists independently of you; it is "out there" for you to find.

Remember the eagle... raise your consciousness!

Holistic success is an ever-evolving and transformative journey. You are always divinely guided, in the present and future-focused, and at the same time, in the next breath, you may have an epiphany that completely alters what you want to create for yourself in your life. Back to our mountain metaphor. When you take on holistic success and become a master of your life, you have embarked on a journey up the mountain, a journey of raising your consciousness.

Now, your success is defined and guided by listening to your soul, your heart's wisdom, and connecting to your intuition and imagination. *Holistic success focuses on who you are and who you are becoming.*

Grounded in your soul observer is where you constitute and define your success. It is the spirit of success, the energetic alignment of who you are with what you want to accomplish. It is not just one aspect of your life; you are now defining and creating your success holistically in all major areas of your life. All of these are aligned with who you are. This shifts your life to being holistically successful and living in internal harmony. This is authentic harmony because it is created from your inner wisdom. This transcends outer world pressures, cultural narratives, and trying to "fit in" at the expense of being true to yourself.

Your success is also created through a multidisciplinary approach. To define your holistic success, you engage with your intuition, imagination, and heart's wisdom to feel your soul's calling and express it in your life. You bring all the elements of your soul observer into creating your success. What is your intuition telling you? What is your imagination showing you? Feel what your purpose, talents, and gifts are to be expressed into the world. You engage your body, emotions, and language to align with the success you define and commit to. Journal, meditate, and have continuous self-awareness that you are in energetic alignment with your success.

This is holistic success. Notice that we have not defined any results commitments, or taken any actions yet. Your transformation into creating and living a holistically successful life is about who you are, at higher levels of consciousness.

This transforms and transcends societal pressures, cultural narratives, unconscious beliefs, and lack and limitation that have defined your life and success. Now, you create what constitutes your success from your true authentic self, in natural alignment with your essence. Now, who you are and your success are in energetic alignment in all areas of your life.

Two different worlds: traditional vs. holistic success.

Again, who versus what is defining your success? Is it your ego or soul observer that defines your success?

Holistic success is your ability to connect to and stay connected to your true authentic self. To listen deeply to your soul to hear and honor your soul's calling. This is where you know, and you know you know... you live with certainty. Your intuition also becomes stronger, which helps you navigate through the cacophony of our world. This keeps you focused and acting with clarity and direction toward fulfilling your purpose and success. Also, listen to your imagination, it, along with your intuition, is how your higher self communicates with you. Honor your imagination, as it holds insights to transform your world.

Holistic success is not to say that when you have success, you do not have the same things as you do with traditional success... not at all. Rather, *it is the context of success about which we are talking.* If you work toward success that is given and defined by social conditioning and the narratives of the past, this is an empty path. The outer, material world path is filled with stress, breakdowns, fear, competition, frustration, and unfulfillment, and leads to dis-ease.

Holistic success is not about what you do. Again, it is about who you are, who you are becoming, and living your life with purpose and fulfillment. It is about having a vision for your life that calls you, inspires (in-spirit) you, and wakes you up in the morning, saying, "Your future is waiting, let's go!" It is your future that you create that calls you, transforming and transcending the limitations of your past.

And it all begins with raising your consciousness. Higher consciousness is what adds self-empowerment to accomplishing your success.

SOAR is not about simply obtaining new levels of success in your life, like you do in traditional success, which is more of a task-based journey void of soul. Now you will have lasting success... and more. As you evolve on your journey of self-mastery, today's level of success will become but a stepping stone to higher levels of your success available to you. Evolution gives choices. As you evolve, you will have choices in how far you want to take your success. Holistic success is always about having harmony in your life and never about gaining success in one area at the expense of others.

The answers to how much holistic success you commit to having in your life reside within you. Your success is now a reflection of your consciousness.

Living your life as your soul observer, with holistic success defined, let's go to our next domain in SOAR, the results domain.

Results

Moving to our fourth domain in SOAR - but the third domain in the application of SOAR - are your results. More accurately said, your results commitments. As we know, achieving success in your life is defined by your ability to accomplish your desired results. But the question arises, what kind of success are we talking about? In the traditional sense, success is mainly defined by the level of power, wealth, and fame one achieves. It is defined by what you *do,* how much money you make, how far you climb the corporate ladder, or gain success in your business. These results are largely, if not completely, focused on "doing," completing tasks, and checking off items on a list. The fundamental element of traditional success is being tactical. This mode of operation tends to be driven by external standards, expectations, and performance metrics that neglect a deeper awareness of yourself. This is you operating, almost, if not totally, from your egoic construct as your observer. It emphasizes action without much, if any, consideration for the connection and alignment with your soul, your intuition, your imagination, your emotions, or the very energy that drives you... your essence. But this way of achieving results often leaves a void, a lack of fulfillment, and a sense of disconnection from your true self.

Holistic success puts your external achievements secondary in your life. They are the *effects* of your success. They reflect your inner essence. The *cause* of your success is *who you are*. Your success is now deeply intertwined with your soul, intuition, imagination, and purpose in life. The results you achieve in holistic success reflect your soul observer and are inclusive of every aspect of your life.

This is not to say that traditional success will give you more material success than holistic success. You can have as much material success as you want if that is still what you want. Holistic success transforms the *context* of your success. It is living your life in harmony, from the inside out, and living in personal alignment across six domains of life: spiritual, physical, personal, financial, professional (or retirement), and relationships.

You now define the results you need to fulfill in order to accomplish your success, knowing that your results are interconnected. Each one represents a vital domain of your life while allowing you to have a life of balance, harmony, peace, joy, and success. And how you have and live a purposeful and fulfilling life.

It is essential to keep in mind that with SOAR, the distinction is that your results commitments are strategies to fulfill your success rather than tactical actions to take. Making goals may be a long-held habit that is well-embedded in your subconscious and a strong habit. To have the holistic success you desire, you must break the tactical actions-results loop of goals and create results commitments aligned with your observer and success domains. This is a contextual and transformative change from traditional goal setting!

Here are the six domains in which to create your results commitments, including their order and holistic success highlights. I invite you to take your time and reflect on each domain as you read them.

> **Spiritual:** This domain involves a deep connection with your soul. It is knowing that you are a spiritual being having a human experience. You are a divine, infinite creator. It is being open and listening to your intuition and imagination. It is your connection to and alignment with something greater than yourself. Religious achievements or practices do not measure results commitments. Instead, results commitments are defined by your soul's wisdom.
>
> What practices can you create, or do you have, to anchor and stay present to your spiritual essence, your divine wisdom?
>
> How can you build and strengthen your soul observer by building your connection to your intuition and imagination?

Physical: Fulfilling your results commitments for your physical well-being is not just about knocking it out at the gym or having fitness goals or health markers. It is about listening to your body, honoring its needs, and ensuring it is energized and aligned with your soul observer. Physical vitality becomes a reflection of your inner harmony, and your results commitments now become a reflection of your body's wholeness.

In this perspective, what comes to mind for you to create results commitments around?

How is the holistic aspect of your physical well-being different from what you know and do today?

Personal: The personal domain encompasses your individual growth, self-care, and the pursuit of activities that fulfill you on a personal level. If you have something you want in your life vision that doesn't fit in the other domains, put it in your personal domain. This is why it is often the most vast domain of our life vision. In a world of thinking we have to do more, do it faster, and better, rest and rejuvenation are important elements to your personal domain. Your results commitments here mean committing to your personal development in ways you feel connected to and honoring your true authentic self. Where you are connected to and aligned with your values, virtues, and your heart's desires.

This is the domain for you to create results commitments to know thyself. What practices can you create to acquire new knowledge that supports your evolution?

List at least three other things that come to mind for you that are new or different from what you have been doing.

Financial: Results commitments in this domain are traditionally measured exclusively by wealth, the amount of money you have. But defining your results commitments now is about the energy you bring to your financial domain. It concerns your relationship with prosperity, abundance, security, and purpose. When you align your financial results commitments with your soul's purpose, finances cease to be a source of stress and instead become a reflection of your inner alignment.

What new result commitment in the domain of prosperity can you create for your life?

When you align your true authentic self with prosperity, what feelings come up for you?

How can you harness your emotions and courage to create more prosperity?

Professional or Retirement: Whether you are actively working or retired, establishing your results commitments now involves how you contribute to the world through your vocation or legacy. And a legacy is not only something you leave. But you can also live a legacy. And the real expression of holistic success is to live and leave a legacy. Defining your results and commitments in this domain includes how you spend time reflecting on your inner values and passions, and what inspires you. It also often includes your desire to make a meaningful impact on your family, friends, and the world.

What results commitments do you need to define and create to achieve holistic success in this domain?

What are you not doing today that your soul has been telling you for quite some time? Is it time to be doing "it?"

Define your purpose in life from your soul, from the depths of your knowing. Divine purpose is deeply inspirational.

Relationships: In this domain, results commitments are not measured by the number of people you know or social achievements, but by the depth and authenticity of your connections. It means your relationships are energetically aligned with love, compassion, understanding, empathy, and mutual support, creating bonds that nourish both parties. What do your results commitments look like that reflect this?

What feelings and emotions can you bring into your most cherished relationships?

If you have a relationship that is in a breakdown, whether the person is in this dimension or not, what result commitment can you create to bring peace and completion, if you need to, or to create a beautiful relationship into existence?

Fulfilling your results commitments is not simply about crossing off milestones in these areas but crafting a life where each domain is energetically aligned with your inner self and reflected in your thoughts, beliefs, feelings, body, emotions, and language. In contrast, traditional success is about doing more, achieving more, and reaching for the ever-changing, fast-paced, uncertain, and temporal external benchmarks.

I invite you to hit your pause button on life once again.

To stop.

To breathe.

Stop for a moment. Reflect on and feel the energetic alignment of what you have created for yourself on your journey of SOARing in your life: your thoughts, feelings, body, emotions, and language, all in the present yet all future-focused.

- What is coming up for you?

- What insights are you having?

- Can you begin to see how to incorporate the transformational strategies of SOAR into your life?

- Are you feeling a new life unfolding for yourself?

- What new, different, or edited results commitments do you have insights on?

Again, you are the author of your success. Your future-focus unlocks your potential. What are you creating for your life? This can be no less than a radical transformation! Feel it, do not think about it.

Are you feeling the holistic aspect of your success unfolding?

Your results commitments. They are a reflection of your inner purpose and divine wisdom. They no longer define you; they reflect who you are. It is the fulfillment of your results commitments that now has you accomplishing success that not that long ago, you could not have imagined. As Yoda so famously said, "Do or do not. There is no try." You are either fulfilling your desired results commitments or not. There is no hiding, excusing, justifying, or ignoring the results you are currently experiencing. In fact:

You are responsible for the results you **are** getting in your life.

You are responsible for the results you **are not** getting in your life.

In our results domain, let's examine how the definition of integrity in SOAR is key to your success. This definition of integrity does not define integrity as a moral issue. Instead, it is a function of workability and performance. Integrity now becomes critical to your ability to fulfill your results commitments.

Integrity

Fulfilling your results commitments is the bottom line that determines the level of holistic success you will achieve in your life. The more effectively and efficiently you can take the necessary actions to fulfill your results commitments, the quicker, easier, and smoother you will achieve your desired holistic success.

Integrity plays a crucial role in your ability to achieve the results you want in life. And when you think of integrity, most people define it in a moral context. While this definition holds true, SOAR defines integrity as a function of being able to fulfill your results commitments. It is your ability to fulfill your results commitments that causes your success. Work as hard and as long as you want, and if you don't get the results you want, you don't get the success you want. The more efficiently you can take the actions to fulfill your results commitments, the easier and quicker your success will come. And to the level you want, the more success you are capable of having.

Said differently, SOAR defines integrity as the performance element to your success.

And a reminder here: We are focused on you as your soul observer, not what you are going to do. It is easy to forget this and fall back into your action domain, ignoring your observer domain.

Grounding yourself in your soul observer, here is the definition of integrity SOAR uses:

Integrity is honoring your word plus being responsible for your results, which equals your level of performance.

Remember, it is your word that gives your world. It is your word that creates your world. It is your word that has the ability to recode your DNA. As a spiritual being, having a human experience, it is your word that is a portal to your holistic success. It is the use of language that you build your self-agency. From a psychological perspective, you gain the wisdom and power to develop self-agency. This is the term used to describe someone solely responsible for their thoughts, feelings, and actions. Being responsible for your results causes integrity to be a conscious and self-empowering component to your success.

There is no space for a victim in this equation. Rather, when you experience a breakdown as a function of your performance, you look at yourself from your soul observer self and reflect on who you are, looking for what is out of alignment or missing that is causing you not to fulfill your desired result commitment. You reflect on your thoughts, beliefs, language, and emotions and see the breakdown as an opportunity for your growth and evolution.

Integrity is aligning your word (observer), success, results commitments, and actions. When all four domains are aligned in the same energy, integrity is another powerful element of your multidisciplinary approach to creating your life.

With the observer, success, and results domains in integrity, in the same spirit of success, feel the energy you have as you embark on taking action! Your external actions create a flow where results manifest not from stress, strain, and the heaviness of tasks, but from the intentionality and clarity of your inner world.

You have also dropped your baggage from the past because you are being forward-focused. Feel the shift in your energy. The shift into experiencing life in higher levels of emotions and consciousness.

Being linguistic beings, we language our success, and we know language has the power to create. When you operate with integrity, energetically, you are creating and holding the space for your success.

You now have a performance element to SOAR in your life. Think of integrity in the context of energy and frequency. The foundation of integrity is your word. Your language domain is a bridge between your inner world and your outer world. Between what you say you want, your success, and the results you get in your life. And you are responsible for your results. No one else is. Nothing else is. Awe... the power of you as your observer self, your true authentic self expressing in your human experience.

I'm reminded of Hermes Trismegistus' famous quote, "As within, so without, as above, so below, as the universe, so the soul."

Integrity plays a key role in your journey, who you are, your success, and to the level of holistic success you commit to. However, the seductive elements of the ego will influence you until they don't. They will pull you back to traditional ways of being, until they don't. Success and self-mastery are non-linear journeys. Sometimes, it will feel like you are on an infinite plateau; try as you may, you don't seem to be evolving. At times, it will feel like you took many steps backward. This is all a natural progression on your journey of evolving and self-mastery. This is where, too often, the emotion of stress can put its limiting grip on you. Stress, viewed from an energetic point of view, limits, constricts, and too often, prevents you from achieving success.

Stress

Today's world is filled with stress, breakdowns, emptiness, and dis-ease. Each one is a crisis unto itself. Stress is a function of our egoic constructs, identification with our mind, thoughts, and roles we play in life. The ego convinces us that stress is unavoidable and essential for our success.

Remember, the ego's purpose: to predict, control, and survive, all coming from our past. It has us believing that without tension or anxiety, we would lose our drive, becoming stagnant, complacent, and unable to be successful. In this mindset, stress feels like fuel for action, as it is a necessary burden to bear to achieve, accomplish, and succeed. Our egos are so attached to pressure, stress, and breakdowns that many people can no longer truly relax. With the ego wanting to survive at all costs and loving to compare and seek agreement with things and people in our world to validate and justify itself, this keeps us chained to our patterns of breakdowns and stress. Most people believe this illusion, unaware that a deeper, more sustainable way of living is available.

We live in the fastest-paced, fastest-changing, most uncertain, technologically advanced, global, fear-based, and materialistic world our history has ever known. I invite you to pause and reflect on this sentence in relation to the previous paragraph.

Do you see and *feel* the disconnect? And see why there is so much disconnect in our world. Do you feel the discordant energy in this? Do you feel the false veil that your ego has you living and believing to be the truth?

Yet most humanity lives connected solely to the material world, void of connection to its inner wisdom, its soul. Its communication line to its intuition is cut off, and its imagination is completely turned off.

Is it any wonder that heart disease is the leading cause of death *in the world for both men and women?* This reflects the amount of stress we have in our daily lives.

There are several articles written on the topic of *stress as the number one killer!* It is stress that is the number one cause of death. It is also known as the proxy killer. It has this name because while people die of heart attacks, strokes, cancer, diabetes, and many other diseases, these are the effects of stress. Stress is the cause; the effect is the fatal disease.

Stress occurs because of the stories we tell ourselves about circumstances, situations, events, and people in our lives. Whether our stories are real or not, our brains do not know the difference and believe our stories to be the truth.

People die because of the stories they tell themselves. Augmenting this, they are also unaware of who they are as their observer: ego or soul. Most people live in an egoic state, unaware they are telling themselves stories. Unaware that they always have the power to declare which observer they are being and then reframe, recontextualize, the stories they are telling themselves. We always have a choice in the meaning we make out of anything in life. A fundamental truth of life is that it is meaningless. We give meaning to life. All of life. And when the ego is in control of a person's life, creating and telling stories about what is happening in their life, causing them to react to their outer world, this is a level of a Michelin chef's recipe for breakdowns, unfulfillment, lack of purpose, and stress to occur. Remember, we tell our stories, but then *we forget they are stories, and we live as though these stories are the truth.*

Also, remember that the ego's sole purpose is to predict, control, and survive, which are all given by your past. If your ego is sitting in the driver's seat of your life, it is in control of your life, and most of your goals and dreams go unfulfilled. Utilizing the SOAR elements in your life, you can transform and transcend the egoic construct. You no longer resign yourself to "life as it is," another favorite belief of the ego. Living in the ego observer has also given cause to the "lack of purpose" crisis in our world today.

Instead of having a purpose in your life, the ego has

142

you, and you are fully vested in the action domain of "what am I going to do?" and believe your stories to be the truth. And what you are going to do could change in the next breath because your actions are not grounded in your purpose. The ego observer is the domain of reacting, doing, problem, challenge, and if it isn't working, what can you *do* differently, mentality.

Said differently, with your ego in your life's driver's seat, your life lacks soul and connection to your heart's wisdom.

Are you clear why stress is a crisis in our world today?

Are you feeling where your stress comes from?

With the knowledge and insights you have gained from SOAR, what can you alter about yourself to transform your stress into self-empowerment?

When you begin your journey of evolving and self-mastery, you discover that holistic success does not feel heavy. Connection to your essence, your soul, guided by your intuition, imagination, and purpose, reveals a life that breaks the chains of stress. This is where you realize that living a life with purpose and fulfillment arises not from the tension of stress but from alignment with your inner wisdom.

We have all witnessed professional or Olympic athletes operate in what is often referred to as the zone. It is also called being in the flow. This is our natural state of harmony, where our inner and outer worlds are coordinated. Where our actions emerge effortlessly, no longer driven by fear or egoic validation, but by our inner wisdom, we alter how time occurs in this state. We have all experienced being so engrossed in a project that hours pass as minutes. This is also where our actions arise intuitively. This is also a state of self-mastery.

Now, you operate in your life with your success reflecting your inner world. You live in the present, yet you are living into your future that you create. In the present, you are future-focused. Remember, forward vision unlocks potential. This is in stark contrast to your egoic construct unconsciously controlling your life.

This is how you overcome stress. Because now you live your life...

- From your soul observer self. Connected to your heart's wisdom and guided by your intuition and imagination.

- In the present.

- Being future-focused.

- With purpose. Purpose aligned with and given by your true authentic self. This is what causes a fulfilling life.

- In the flow of life, with your inner and outer worlds in harmony.

Now you have focus.

Now you have clarity.

Now you have direction.

Now you have velocity.

Imagine a life where you fulfill your results commitments with joy, harmony, grace, and ease. Living in alignment with your true authentic self, stress becomes obsolete. This is because you no longer rely on, or are defined by, the external pressures and expectations of societal norms, culture, and traditions. This is where you are inspired to fulfill your results commitments instead of being fueled by the temporary motivation of the outside world. Your energy is guided by the wisdom of your intuition and imagination, with your soul guiding you to be true to your authentic self.

While problems and challenges will arise, you will no longer feel overwhelmed and fall into breakdowns because you are no longer meeting the problems and challenges that occur from the ego's perspective. You transcend the fear and scarcity that the ego feeds on. Instead, you embrace problems, challenges, and breakdowns as opportunities for growth, knowing that life supports you when you move with it.

Observer: ego, small, divisive self or soul, intuition, and imagination. You always have the power of choice.

SOAR is experiential. It works only if you embody what it has to offer. But from wherever you begin your journey to self-mastery, your life can sometimes seem daunting, with many setbacks. The ego is capable of being very covert and sneaky when feeling threatened. This is why you must build and strengthen your soul observer to overcome the egoic construct. Also, become aware that most of us for our entire lives have, and are living, a life given by our ego observer. This gives your ego observer a lot of practice in being who it is. It is critical to know and understand this, as it will take time and perseverance to live as your soul observer at the same level as you live from the ego observer today.

The following intangible results can help you build and strengthen your soul observer. Reflect on the previous *Levels of Learning and Competence* section to help you understand where you are with each one. Consciously be and stay aware that this is your journey of evolving, ever evolving, in life. Also, be mindful of transformational learning and avoid falling into the habitual patterns of the past, thinking, "What am I going to do?" Instead, anchor to and reflect from your soul observer, "Who am I?"

Intangible Results

When people think of success, they often focus on the tangible things they want, such as buying a new house, securing a promotion, or making a certain income level. These results are easy to define and track, offering a clear roadmap in our pursuit of our external, outer world, validation. While they are valid things to strive for in our journey of success, they are only part of the story. Becoming mindful of the intangible and subjective results in your life is building and strengthening your soul observer.

Intangible results are highly personal, influencing, defining, and establishing the context of who you are. We can call intangible results a "life mastery bridge," as they give the context and content of your physical reality.

I invite you to reflect, go within, on the intangible results that you would like to add to how you define your success and the subsequent results you are committed to fulfilling.

Also, reflect on the results commitments you currently have for yourself, your outer world subjective results. For example, making a certain income level, reaching a level of professional success, driving a certain car, defining the relationships you have in your life, or living in a certain home in a certain neighborhood. Whatever results you are currently committed to

148

obtaining, reflect on them in the context of your intangible results.

As your soul observer, consciously connect to your heart's wisdom, your divine intelligence. Listen to your intuition and imagination.

Be still and just breathe for a moment.

Do you feel the alignment or the discordant energy between your higher self and your current goals?

Ask yourself why you have the desires you have. Why do you want those "things" in your life and that level of success, however you define success?

Intangible results help shape and define what you do and want. They also keep you focused on creating holistic success. To live your life with fulfillment, peace, a sense of purpose, security, and freedom, to name a few examples.

Understanding this interplay between intangible and tangible results will shift your focus from merely working to achieve your goals (traditional task-focused success) to a profound shift toward holistic success. Your success now will be defined not by what you accumulate but by *who you are and who you are becoming.*

Reminder: Your outer world is but a reflection of your inner world.

As you continue to build your SOARing life, here are examples of intangible results for you to consider having in your life:

Increased Self-Awareness: Remember that all transformation begins with self-awareness. Create a habit of bringing your unconscious to consciousness. To question why you are feeling the way you are, doing what you are doing, or believing you "have to" do whatever that is. Becoming self-aware is your opportunity to challenge, *with discernment, not judgment,* your history, culture, traditions, beliefs, and habits, to break the limiting constraints they hold over you. To search for understanding of who you are as a unique and evolving being. Becoming aware of and deepening your knowledge of your thoughts, feelings, body, emotions, and language, and how they shape your life. This involves your quest to connect to your authentic being, not as a noun but as a dynamic verb, something you are perpetually becoming. This is the journey of self-mastery.

Deepen your Intuition: Take the time and become more aware of your intuition and inner instincts. Intuition is a natural aspect of who each one of us is. Honor it. Strengthen it. Your gut has its own intelligence; listen to it. Your heart was meant to be the master, your brain the servant; listen also to the

150

wisdom of your heart. Your intuition does not compete for space; you must be still and listen. It is always there, available, and willing to share its wisdom. This is the domain of the source of your insights.

Humility: Show up in life in your greatness, as your true authentic self, but always with humility. *Humility is a superpower.* Our world, the egoic construct, believes hubris is our superpower. Nothing could be further from the truth. When, in the bible, it says to be like a child to enter heaven. Heaven is a state of consciousness, not a place to go to. And why children? Why be like a child to get into a higher state of consciousness? Children are open, curious, and humble. In the emotion of humility, you are open and curious. You know you don't know far more than you know. Hubris believes just the opposite. Be your authentic superpower.

Emotional Maturity and Resilience: Emotions are energy in motion. Emotions, as energy, exist in frequencies. An easy way to view and understand this is with the metaphor of an elevator. The down buttons represent low vibration emotions such as greed, envy, jealousy, and anger. Conversely, the up buttons represent emotions such as acceptance, joy, happiness, bliss, compassion, and gratitude. Our emotional domain is rich beyond measure. Begin to see emotions not as good or bad but as signposts pointing to what you care about. Be open to learning and understand what emotions bring to you as messages, lessons, and gifts. Also, build your ability to recover quickly from breakdowns and any circumstance, situation, event, or what someone says or does with your emotions. Most importantly, with emotions and moods, you manage them, never control them, and as your divine self, you *always have the ability to create and manage your emotions and never unconsciously react with your emotions. Instead, you consciously respond inside of the emotion you create.*

Inner Peace: Connected to your heart's wisdom, knowing you create your world, commit to achieving a consistent state of calm and inner peace… regardless of external stimulus. This is self-mastery. Knowing who you are, your true authentic self, and being connected to it causes you to be peaceful. Being in a peaceful state also brings a reward anytime life throws something at you, and you experience a breakdown. When you are peaceful, you stay open to dealing with the breakdown. Keep your thoughts, feelings, body, emotions, and language in the energy of peace. This allows you to connect to and stay connected to your inner wisdom. Now you can think clearly and rationally to respond into the outer world circumstances, situations, events, and people.

Clarity of Purpose: We all come into this lifetime with gifts, talents, and treasures. You find and live your life purposefully by connecting with your heart's wisdom and soul and listening to your intuition and imagination. A purposeful life gives a fulfilling life. The highest calling we have is to find our purpose and then be of service to others through our purpose.

Compassion: Compassion is one of the highest emotions we are capable of. It is the gateway to transformation and transcendence in your life on the path of self-mastery. The place, often overlooked, to begin with compassion is with yourself. Compassion allows you to shift your perspective from judgement to inquiry. From resisting, that which you resist persists, to acceptance. You now see life as a mirror; that which you give, you get. Perceived mistakes, failures, and suffering are not seen as insurmountable obstacles, but rather as messengers inviting you to look for the gifts they hold. Compassion comes with self-awareness and self-observation. These are the two doors to freedom. Living life with self-compassion, you engage with life with curiosity, being open, and grace.

Showing compassion for others stems from your awareness that we are all on a unique journey in life. Everyone is at a different level on the mountain and is in the process of evolving. Some people are stuck in an egoic construct with no desire to be different and get to see and experience their world from the valley. Other people climb the mountain to the summit to view and experience life from higher levels of consciousness, giving different views and perspectives of life. In our commitment to our own compassion, we now understand that everyone is always doing the best they can. We do not know the whole story of the other person, regardless of how close they are to us.

Compassion provides clarity and direction for living with purpose. When we see life through the eyes of compassion, both toward ourselves and others, we become attuned to the deeper purpose underlying our experiences. Purpose, in this sense, is not an external destination but an inner alignment with the flow of life.

Other Centric: This is also called being altruistically selfish. Defining our purposes in life and knowing who we are, it is reflected in our outer world; we engage in the fundamental law of reciprocity. This is often described as, "As you give, you get." The law of reciprocity always works, but with SOAR, you consciously harness its power and bring it into your life. Living in an other centric way, listening, caring, and acting in service to others, transforms your life. It helps and supports you in achieving a fulfilling and purposeful life. When you have empathy and compassion and show that you care for the well-being of others, people, and nature, this reflects the most fundamental element of life: we are all One. Being altruistically selfish helps others achieve their results commitments, and in doing so, you fulfill your results commitments. Also, it is for us to be an example of what being of service means and to act for the betterment of all.

This is living life in the flow, in the energy of "as you give, you get." Knowing that giving and receiving are the same energy, you are sowing the seeds of your future prosperity with every act of caring, appreciation, and generosity. Being other-centric, combined with generative language, is the super fuel for the actions we now take.

Once you have connected yourself to your soul observer, being other-centric is the most powerful, transformative, transcendent, and humbling thing you can do to live a fulfilling and purposeful life. Being other-centric means understanding that our true purpose unfolds not in isolation but through connection, service, caring, and contribution. Yes, it is "as you give you get." But that is not the whole story. To be of service is how you grow. When you uplift others, you uplift yourself. This is the essence of the flow of your life: giving, receiving, and becoming. It is yet another aspect of the journey of self-mastery.

Gratitude: Our egos only know scarcity, lack, limitation, division, and survival. Transforming your life to live in gratitude is not the "be positive" mentality. Instead, it is a state of consciousness. A generative state of consciousness where you navigate the journey of your evolving, success, and self-mastery, seeing new possibilities and opportunities you previously could not see. You know what is present to work with instead of what is missing. This transcends the egoic construct's scarcity, victimhood, and fear mentality. Gratitude is an inside job, without regard to what is showing up in your outer world. It is a reflection of you as your observer self.

Energetically, you are aligned with abundance and prosperity. What you focus on expands, and gratitude becomes the vibration that harmonizes your consciousness with the infinite creative potential of the universe. This reminds us that we are spiritual beings having a human experience, and gratitude is a high vibration emotion. One of the lenses of gratitude is that it gives us the knowing that life is happening through us, not to us. This keeps us aligned and connected to our essence, centered, and grounded. When gratitude becomes who you are, this leads to greater success in life and a deeper connection with others, nature, and your soul.

I AM: The ultimate declaration of being. It is declaring your highest truth: you are a spiritual being having a human experience. This is the ultimate in generative language when you declare I AM (and whatever words follow). You are generating into the world; your word gives your world. I AM is an act of creation. When you act from your soul observer self and declare I AM..., you are tapped into the creative forces of the multiverse and creating what you declare into your life. When you say I AM, you define who you are and call forth the essence of what you wish to embody. You become the bridge between spirit and physical, between potential and reality.

When you truly understand the transformative power of I AM, you stop passively navigating through life based on your past stories, societal, cultural, and traditional labels, norms, and expectations. Instead, you live as a creator, and we are all infinite, divine creators, grounded in the present moment and declaring your future into existence. I AM holds the potential to awaken the power to create and live fully, allowing you to create any level of holistic success you wish.

Reflect on the earlier section about **stress** (page 140). Take time to understand it and uncover the stories you are living in your life that are causing your stress. Create ways to support yourself as your soul observer and be grateful for the lessons and gifts the stress teaches you. And with this new awareness, how can you, as your soul observer, transform and transcend your stress? Also, how can you create an environment that supports and calls you to your new stress-free life?

Build your Integrity: This is not a moral issue but a function of workability and performance. It means what we say and do are all aligned. When breakdowns occur, we look for a break in workability, not as a punishment or as having done something wrong. We look at ourselves to see where the breaks or disconnects in our thoughts, beliefs, and feelings are occurring. Imagine tuning a musical instrument. If one string is off, the whole composition is compromised. Likewise, when we act out of alignment with our purpose, our true authentic self, our deepest truths, we disrupt the energy of our lives. Integrity is not a heavy, moral issue. Instead, it is an invitation to live authentically. In this context, it is not something we practice, but rather it is who we become. Integrity is a foundational element of one's performance levels and holistic success.

Build Your Communication Skills: As human beings, we are linguistic beings. You actively shape the world you live in through your language. Your language and your communication skills are both a mirror and a portal. Language creates your reality. What you put out comes back to you, life's mirror. The portal gives you the power to create your life through communication. Mastering communication skills has nothing to do with learning vocabulary or structure. It is about mastering your internal dialogue and self-talk. When you fail to use language intentionally, you trap yourself in your past. Your past stories of lack, limitations, struggles, challenges, and breakdowns. When you consciously build your communication skills, you create your success. Cultivating your communication skills defines and causes your success. But your success isn't the outcome of doing in the action's domain; your success is who you are in language. Your level of success becomes a natural consequence of your ability to speak your future into existence. Cultivating your communication skills is also illuminating your path to self-mastery.

Personal Growth: We live in the most uncertain and fastest-changing world in history. We are also infinite, spiritual beings having a human experience. The largest body of knowledge is what we don't know we don't know. This is especially true of Socrates's words, "Know thyself." Immanuel Kant wrote that knowing oneself should be "an ethical commandment to know one's own heart and to understand the motives behind one's actions, in order to harmonize one's will with one's duty." Being a lifelong student of Self is the journey of evolving and self-mastery.

Intangible results are you building and strengthening the connection to your inner world, your essence, and your soul. This is building and strengthening your soul observer. This is who you are and who you are becoming. They are major elements in creating the foundation for your success and life. They are your guides to your thoughts, perceptions, feelings, beliefs, and emotional well-being. They also alter the starting point of how you deal with issues and people in your life. Your external world does not measure the fulfillment of your intangible results by the standards of our ever-changing, uncertain, temporal world. But rather, they are measured by the level of connection you are experiencing in your life to your true authentic self. To your soul. To hear your intuition, your divine wisdom, speak to you. This is where you create and live authentically, grounded in your beingness, which allows you to create a life of deep meaning, and from your inspiration, which is beyond the material world.

This is holistic success.

This is evolving.

This is self-mastery.

Remember, as we give, we get. This is a Law of the Universe. When your inner world is grounded in and connected to your intangible results and commitments, they cause you to live your life in *higher-level energies.* This is what you are giving to the world. This is what you will get from the world. The Laws of Attraction and Cause and Effect always work and support you. Creating a combination of these intangible results in your life is how you connect your inner and outer worlds. They are a bridge to your holistic success.

Are you feeling the transformative power and the possibilities these intangible results hold for you?

This may be a good time to hit the pause button on life and take some time to journal. Reflect on new insights you became aware of as you read this section.

From intangible results to tangible results. This is another bridge between subjective experience and objective reality: the dance between being and doing, spirit and structure, potential and practice.

With your intangible results defined and their importance to your holistic success understood, let's keep building your foundation and discussing creating your physical reality.

Tangible Results

The way we perceive and engage with life holds immense power. Again, your intangible results are fundamental and serve as a foundational element for your life. They are your "life mastery bridge." Intangible results cause the context of your tangible results. When your intangible and tangible results are energetically in alignment, this is your path to holistic success, evolving, and self-mastery.

Tangible results are your results commitments in your physical world. They are the same as goals in traditional success. But you now know the power of a commitment versus a goal, and why in SOAR, tangible results are results commitments. But here is another transformational aspect of your tangible results. They align with your inner world. Your inner clarity translates into choices for your success and subsequent results commitments. It is not enough to hold empowering beliefs or develop new ways of seeing; we must also engage in the world and take actions that reflect our inner world. Your success now reflects who you are and who you are becoming. As within, so without, is now aligned. This is where transformation becomes real, where you step beyond ideas and beliefs and into a life designed and lived consciously.

Let me offer a metaphor for intangible and tangible results and building a car. Let's say you are a master auto craftsman, designer, and engineer, just like you are learning self-mastery by learning SOAR.

Imagine yourself standing in the middle of a super-large building. And in that building, there are the parts needed to build any car you can imagine. Being a master car craftsman, designer, and engineer, you know the components necessary to build a car and how to do it. Taking on learning and mastering SOAR, and connected to and guided by your inner world, you can build any life you want for yourself. SOAR gives you all the components to build any life you want.

Embarking on building your car, you ponder what is possible. What car have you dreamt of that you can now turn into reality? No limitations, what is possible in building your dream car? Because of your skill level with automobiles, you have the distinct advantage of being able to dream and envision things in your car that others cannot see. And your skillset allows you to turn your dream car into reality.

On your journey of SOAR, you will evolve and develop new dreams and envision things for your life that you cannot see today. You are also expanding your skill set to be able to turn your new dreams into reality. As you grow and evolve, your dreams of today will be replaced by new dreams. Dreams that align with who you have become and who you are becoming.

Building your dream car may appear to be easier than transforming your life because it is grounded in the question, "What do I need to do?" You have the skills, you create the plans, and the parts and components are at hand to make whatever you dream possible. Beyond the initial stage of designing a car, where everything is possible, it becomes essentially a task project.

In contrast, creating any life you want may seem like a daunting dream. But when you live as your soul observer, your life transforms, and you transcend. The ultimate journey of life is to live connected to your soul. We are divine, God makes no mistakes, and there are no accidents. The fact that you, I, and everyone exist is proof of our perfection and our divine self. SOAR is your blueprint to connecting to your true authentic self and consciously creating your life, your outer world as a reflection of your innate virtues, talents, and gifts. Just like the metaphor of building a car, where the only limitation is your imagination, so too with SOAR and your life. The only limitation is your imagination.

Knowing very well the components of a car, and what is possible, do you haphazardly throw parts together and hope for the best? When you hit the start button, do you hope it will start, or do you have the certainty that the car will work perfectly? Do you take the time to plan what you will create consciously? Are you very specific about what you are designing and building?

Do you take the time as the master craftsman you are to craft, design, tweak, and change things along the way as you construct a vehicle that becomes beyond what you can imagine today? You can do this because of your mastery of designing and building cars.

With SOAR as your transformational blueprint and foundation, guiding you in a multidisciplinary approach, you can build a life beyond what you can imagine today. As big or small as you want, do anything you want, have anything you want. All of this is on your journey of evolving to self-mastery.

And you are the author of your success.

And you are the architect of your future.

What life are you going to create for yourself, divine creator?

Just like having blueprints to build your perfect car, SOAR is the blueprint for your ideal future and holistically successful life. It is where you turn your dreams, hopes, and desires into your perfect life reality.

Being a spiritual being having a human experience, today, you can only "see," envision, perceive, understand, and comprehend your life at the level of consciousness you are in. This is the premise of cognitive dissonance. This is true for all of us. When you embark on the journey of SOARing in your life, you've embarked on a journey of being a lifelong student of life, evolving, and self-mastery. Remember, a master is a teacher who never stopped being a student. This is a journey of raising your consciousness. As you raise your consciousness, your thoughts, perspectives, what you can envision, perceive, understand, beliefs, values, and insights all change. They align with your higher states of consciousness. Raising your consciousness can be likened to comparing the views when standing in the valley between the mountains and on the summit of a mountain.

Wrapping up our metaphor, are you allowing your car to be whatever you throw together? Assembling your car with little or no purpose? With no final plan as to what the result will be? If you built a car this way, you quickly see that it may look more like something that belongs to a contemporary art museum than a fine-tuned, extraordinary vehicle. Yet, this is precisely how most people live, *without* plans and a purpose. And without purpose, you react to circumstances, situations, events, and people. This is where people live primarily in descriptive language, describing how life is happening *to them*. In contrast, are you, divine creator, creating, designing, building your life that is everything, and more, of which you have dreamed? Where you live in the flow of life, with life happening through you.

With the teachings of SOAR, you now have a fundamental foundation that is built on and created from your soul observer. Your intangible results reflect this. Your life becomes about evolving, a never-ending process of raising your consciousness. Life now is also a never-ending process of having to edit and revise what success is for you and your results commitments to fulfill your new levels of success. Remember, SOAR is your fundamental foundation that you can never outgrow because it reflects your level of consciousness. And you are authoring your success. Build a tiny home or a castle, SOAR will support any level of success you create for yourself. You can't outgrow the wisdom of your soul. This is defining your success and your enlightened journey to self-mastery.

Most people focus on and live primarily in the domains of tangible results and actions. So, creating this domain for yourself is likely an easy exercise. However, I want to offer some tangible results for you to consider because you have altered the context of your success. Stay mindful of this as you create and define the tangible results you are committed to fulfilling. For example, you may still have the same goals as you did with traditional success. But evolving into holistic success, you now have results commitments, not goals, and have raised your consciousness, creating tangible results from your soul observer consciousness instead of being driven by external pressures.

Here are several domains as examples of tangible results you may want to use for your holistic success:

Spiritual Connection and Growth: You may think that spirituality is not tangible. You are correct. But you are a spiritual being having a human experience. To create tangible results in this domain is grounding your spiritual, true authentic self into your physical reality. What practices can you bring into your life that keep you connected and grounded to your spiritual self? Journaling, meditation, and breathwork are three great examples to engage in. Being a spiritual being having a human experience, your spiritual domain is the most critical element of SOAR. This is how you live from your essence, being true to your soul, your soul's calling, and being able to hear the "still small voice," your intuition. It is where you also connect with your imagination, which is the insight into your future life.

Financial Security: Transforming your financial domain is likely the most challenging. God and money are probably the two words with the most definitions and baggage in the English language.

Our world is steeped in defining, in a large part, if not totally, that the size of one's net worth equals their success. In the traditional success model, we are rewarded when we have a lot of money, and it is acceptable that we lack character and morals, have several broken relationships, and compromise our health on the journey to dollars in the bank. Achieving holistic success puts no limits on the size of your financial house. Instead, it is a shift in the context of your finances. It is not just money, but prosperity, that SOAR teaches. Also, the definition of money in SOAR is help. The level of help or service you provide to others is reflected in your level of compensation.

In our world today, money is our medium of exchange. Determining how much money you need as income and savings to provide dignity in retirement is the fundamental element of your financial success. Another essential component of your financial security is creating your financial domain before your professional domain in your life vision, ensuring you can achieve your financial results commitments with your current profession, and have a dignified retirement.

Physical Well-being: Although you are a spiritual being having a human experience, your body is how you navigate through life. Your body carries your soul through your life's journey. Taking care of your body helps you navigate and experience life more easily and accomplish more. When you live connected to and aligned with your true authentic self, your body is open and functions better. In fact, it takes a *lot* of energy to live in the egoic construct. The egoic construct drains your energy. In contrast, it is a natural out picturing of who you are to live in love, compassion, and gratitude. Transcending the egoic construct and low energy emotions heals your body and increases your energy. Remember, emotions are energy in motion. If emotions are suppressed and repressed, they will manifest in your body as breakdowns and dis-ease. And the power of your language also influences your body's well-being. Remember, divine creator, you have the power through your language to recode your DNA. Knowing how your emotions and language influence your body is a rare and advanced skill in life!

Cost: Understanding the four elements of cost allows you to become much more aware of the ways in which cost can and does rob you of your success. Time and money are the two most popular elements of cost. Also, the only two elements that many people define cost by. However, perhaps more important than the first two elements is the third element: your energy. You invest your energy in everything you do. Whether you are operating in low or high energy, greed, or compassion. Augmenting the energy element is the time you spend in these energies. More time, more energy. The fourth element of cost is one that few know about, and fewer consider it a cost factor. This fourth element of cost is lost opportunity. You invest your money, time, and energy into things you do. If what you invest in is not in pursuit of fulfilling your life vision, your holistic success, of being true to your soul, then whatever you have exchanged your money, time, and energy for is a lost opportunity in fulfilling, by your definition, your success. And you may be thinking, "Do I have to be doing something all the time? Where do I get a chance to chill, to take a break?" That is a fair question and a concern. But in the definition of holistic success, you live your life in harmony where rest, relaxation, rejuvenation, and entertainment are all included.

Career Advancement: First, you will learn that if you take my *Life Vision to Mastery* program, you create your financial life vision *before* your career life vision. Consider, do your financial goals align with your career goals? Do you want to move into a new profession, follow your intuition, or have a suppressed dream? Or do you want to advance? If so, how far, within your current profession? Perhaps it is creating passive income, turning a hobby into a career, or starting your own business. So many of us are taught that we should pursue a specific career. Fire, police, and military people take pride (pride always comes from your past) in how many generations have been in the profession. We are taught by societal norms, cultures, and traditions what professions one should pursue. Outside influences guide us, and often unconsciously, to choose our profession. The influences of our outer world make us choose our profession, with most often no thought given to whether the profession is aligned with our soul's calling. Your soul knows, be still and listen to its guidance.

Business Growth: If you are or want to become self-employed, what does that look like? If you're in a profession where you can increase your business, such as a salesperson, what does that feel like for you? Do you have a hobby or a passion you desire to turn into your own business? When you are connected to your soul observer and reflecting on the applicability of this domain, at the least, you will experience a contextual shift in how you define business growth. Don't assume you know the answers here. Apply the multidisciplinary elements to SOAR, reflecting, surrendering, and being in silence, for example, be open to hearing the answers. Traditional success elements still apply. Perhaps you want to buy a business or expand your current one. Achieving certain milestones, revenue growth, market share, or expansion into new markets are more examples to ponder. But if these hold true for you, notice their contextual shift. Notice your change from the traditional success mindset to the holistic success mindset. This awareness alters you to your soul.

Your Home: Are you buying your first home, renovating your home, or buying a new home? Moving to a new location, around the block, or around the world? Is it paying off your mortgage? You buy a house; you make it your home. What is home for you? This is critically important, as your home is your environment. Your environment supports you, or not, in being holistically successful. In your evolutionary journey, remain present to how your home environment supports you. Always be mindful of how your home environment is supporting you. A personal example of this I will share with you. I love my library. I love the old-fashioned look, texture, and feel of books. This week, I woke up one morning, looked at my library, and said, "This is just not flowing." So, once again, I have rearranged my books to reflect the ongoing evolution of my consciousness.

For a sampling of my library, please go to **omspiritualcenter.com/sacred-readings-wisdom**, where you can find a list of books to help you on your self-mastery journey.

Family or Personal Milestones: Getting married, having children, doing things with grandchildren, or creating meaningful relationships. Take time to go deep into the meaning of relationships with those closest to you. What do those relationships look like? Do you do things with certain people because they are special to you? Conversely, are there people in your life who are high cost, and you may want to consider ending the relationship(s)? Remember, you are the author of your future. Defining who you have relationships with and what those relationships look like is essential to your holistic success. This also includes two very distinct types of relationships. First, people who you were close to and have died, and you have unresolved issues with them. Second are broken relationships. If either of these types of relationships applies to you, it is time to heal them.

Remember, it is holistic success, which requires harmony in all domains of your life.

Time Freedom: Time is our biggest commodity and one of our most prized possessions. In today's fast-paced world, we have a crisis of a lack of time. Or so the mantra goes with many people. Reflect on this belief, "I don't have time." First, you always have time to do what is most important to you. Always. Second, your heart has a rhythm. It is your timekeeper. Telling yourself you don't have time is aligning yourself with heart dis-ease. Language manifests: here is a critical awareness of your physical well-being. Using the principles of SOAR, especially the four cost elements, how can you restructure your life to have more free time? More time to focus on what you love, including family time? How can you have a work-life balance that is best for you? How can you bring harmony of time into your life and accomplish more? To offer insight into accomplishing this, begin with the mindset that it has already happened! Feel it, language from this place, create your emotions as if you have already achieved plenty of time in your life, and only then, create this for yourself. If you want to have more time, wanting is its own state. If you want, you will get more wanting.

Education and Personal Development: Living in the fastest changing, fast-paced, most technologically advanced, and uncertain world in history, becoming a lifelong learner has become a necessity. The critical place to focus on is being a lifelong learner to know thyself. Given the extreme distractions coming from our world today, the multidisciplinary aspect of SOAR helps you to know yourself better. To know yourself is how you have a peaceful, joyful, fulfilling, purposeful, and successful life. Whether it is your personal or professional domain that you are learning and growing in will change over time. But being mindful of what is important to you and rising above the cacophony in our world today is critical for your holistic success. Dancing between your evolution and your professional education is ongoing. Your intuition and imagination know, be still, and listen.

Travel and Experiences: Maybe you desire to travel and experience different cultures and history? Or having unique experiences, such as skydiving or scuba diving. What dreams of travel and experiences do you hold that you can turn into your reality? Perhaps it is time to combine a hobby or passion with your financial and travel domain to create a new profession?

Safety: When this is missing, little else matters. This can be physical, emotional, or mental safety.

Charitable Giving and Social Impact: Donating your time, money, resources, and talent to causes you care about. Perhaps there is something special to you, and you create your charitable project.

Retirement Planning: Planning today for tomorrow is critical to living your retirement years with peace of mind, quality of life, and dignity. But even if you are in your sixties, it isn't too late. Abraham Lincoln, Louise Hay, and Colonel Sanders are all examples of people who blossomed later in life. I was listening to a podcast recently, and the story of an 80-year-old guy creating a new profession for himself because of his outlook on life! The most critical element in retirement planning is always to have a purpose. And when your purpose comes from your inner world, it knows no limits.

Legacy Planning: Do you want to leave a legacy, live a legacy, or both? Most people think of legacy as leaving a legacy. Living a legacy is being altruistically selfish! Living and leaving a legacy is "having your cake and being able to eat it too."

You define your success by the results you say you want and their fulfillment. Now you know this includes both your intangible and tangible results in life!

But now, all your results commitments reflect who you are. They are in alignment with your success and your soul observer.

In the spirit of your success, you now have a tremendous foundation for launching yourself into the action domain in all areas of your life.

Actions

Having energetically aligned your observer, success, and results domains, it is time to take action to manifest your success.

The action domain is the primary domain for most of us. It is the mindset of doing: "What do I need to do?" "What can or should I do?" The mass consciousness mindset is doing, and if your actions don't work, the focus remains on seeking something different to do. The actions being taken are mostly task-oriented, lacking depth in strategy.

We take the exponential and transformational shift in our lives by moving into the action domain. *This is where we leap from our inner world - observer - to our outer world - actions.* Actions are the how, the tactical, domain. The observer, success, and results domains are the why, context, and strategy.

Your journey into the action domain begins with the understanding that you have altered the context of your actions. You go from being task-focused, in the traditional sense, to being heart-centered and taking actions guided by your soul observer. Instead of actions being task-oriented, and often in the problem-challenge domain (more on this coming up), they become natural actions for you to take. Your actions now become an extension and the effect of who you are. As your soul observer, being energetically aligned with your results commitments, and success domain becomes the cause of your actions. They now occur naturally as things to do, fueled by your purpose and inspiration. This is a transformational shift in why and how you take actions.

The journey of traditional success is centered in the action's domain: "What do I have to do to get what I want?" is the mantra. Now you know that who you are is the cause of your actions. Being connected to and grounded in your inner wisdom causes your actions. Actions now become the effect.

On the journey of traditional success, whether as simple as going out for a meal or designing a yacht, invariably, the first question everyone seems to ask is "What am I going to do?" Knowing what you have already learned about the SOAR model, what is missing in this question?

You are!

The observer! You as your soul observer!

When you begin by asking, "What am I going to do?" This *assumes* that you are showing up with everything in your observer domain nailed, in place, perfected, aligned to your desired result, consciously mindful of, and connected to your desired outcome. This is a blend of egoic hubris, lack of humility, and ignorance. Unless and until you consciously become aware of your observer self and choose who you are that is showing up, you are operating unconsciously, most likely from your egoic construct, and acting out of habit and memory.

You can now begin to see why, in the corporate environment, studies show that about 20% of salespeople sell as much as the other 80%. Over 50% of all goals set go unfulfilled. Only about 24% of salespeople hit their sales goals… and all of this is considered normal!

Continuous improvement programs abound worldwide. They are a complex set of processes and systems, problem-challenge-focused, focused on what to do, on what actions to take to improve "the system." In the traditional sense, this is all about doing… do, do, do. And if that does not work, what can you do differently?

Despite our "modern world," stress and disease are *major* factors in our modern-day lives. In the context of business, they cost us billions of dollars a year. Yet, in the traditional model of success, the focus is on how much more money, fame, and power one can have. It's never-ending.

Doesn't this beg questions such as, "If these steps, processes, and systems are so good, why do most of them fall short or fail to accomplish their desired outcomes?" "Why does the pharmaceutical industry

make almost 1.5 trillion dollars (2022) annually?!"
"Why is there so much stress, breakdowns, fear, and disease in our world today?" To its credit, a lot has been accomplished in our modern world by figuring out what to do. But again, at a cost. Figuring out what to do is the domain of traditional learning, which we will cover shortly. But believing the action domain is the sole domain to get your desired results… would be like judging the cake by tasting a sprinkle on the top of the frosting on the cake… it is just not an accurate assessment of the cake.

Are you seeing the disconnect to success? Are you feeling the discordant energy of traditional success?

This is the cause of people being in crises of lack of purpose, having addictions, and our world being in a crisis in every primary domain of our existence.

Humanity lacks a conscious connection with their soul, with their soul observer.

Look at addictions as an example of the lack of soul in today's success. Addictions are out of control. Get present to the many, many domains in which a person can express themselves with their addictions; alcohol, a plethora of drugs, gambling, shopping, sex, entertainment, the list goes on.

Our industrialized, modern world has been created and lives by the motto of "more, better, and faster."

This is a world completely anchored in the domain of action. While the world has and is seeing amazing technological advances, what is the cost of these technological advancements? The cost relative to our physical and emotional well-being? Not to mention the cost to nature.

Dissatisfaction, stress, anxiety, fear, despair, and resignation abound in the workplace and our lives. The "more, better, and faster" way of being dismisses the human aspect; I don't care what you think or how you feel; just give me more, do it better, and faster.

Living disconnected from our soul and the "more, better, faster" motto is the root cause of stress and dis-ease.

Again, could it be that the modern world has forgotten that we are human beings, not human doings or human havings?

How often have you experienced that no matter how hard you try, no matter what you do, no matter what, the results you say you want simply elude you? Why? Like gravity, there is a direct correlation between you, as the observer, and the actions you take and the results you get. With gravity and this correlation, you do not have to know about it, like it, or understand how and why it works, but they are both always working and affecting our lives. Consciously being aware of this, or not, does not change the fact that the actions you take directly reflect who you are and the results you are getting.

Said differently, your "Beingness," who you are, and your level of consciousness cause the actions you take or do not take and the results you get or don't get.

Our beliefs drive our behaviors. Behaviors are the actions we take and how we take them. Behaviors are both what we do and what we say. This is also, and again, where generative and descriptive language come into play. Generative language is action, causing something to happen. Descriptive language does not move you toward getting results and fulfilling your life vision.

This is an excellent point for reflection. To reflect on your life and see what is driving you.

- Why are you seeking the success you do?

- What cultural and societal narratives are influencing your life?

- Do you feel a disconnect with your inner wisdom?

Understanding that despite your best attempts to take the "perfect" actions, life doesn't always show up as all roses. There are, at times, thorns in life to deal with. They are called breakdowns. Breakdowns occur when we don't fulfill a result commitment, our plans fall apart, or things are not working out. The lack of fulfillment can be stated as a problem or challenge. This is when things seem insurmountable or feel stuck in cycles of frustration. When we feel stuck or can't seem to move off the plateau we are on, caught in cycles of repetition without results, we are on the problem–challenge carousel.

Problem - Challenge Carousel

The problem–challenge carousel is a pervasive issue in all areas of our lives today. This type of breakdown is not random. Life seems like a carousel, with you fixing one problem, another challenge arises, you deal with the new challenge, another problem arises, and things aren't working as planned. It drains your energy and can easily wear you out. It can cause one to feel the burden of stress, frustration, and resignation. "Why try? It's not going to work out anyway" becomes the motto. With people mostly, if not entirely, operating from the action domain with no regard for the observer domain, we set ourselves up for this ride. And the cost in all four domains of SOAR is staggering.

We often do not recognize that the root cause of these breakdowns lies not in what we are doing but in who we are and who is doing the doing. This is the fuel that keeps the carousel spinning. When we focus solely on external actions, we miss the deeper opportunity these breakdowns present. Breakdowns present a chance to go within and reflect on how our consciousness is creating and shaping our experiences.

We take action to get our desired results. Our commitments and intentions drive desired results. If the action worked, you feel a sense of accomplishment and keep going. And this is that sense of flow when things work as planned that we aim for. However, when our actions didn't work, we didn't get our desired outcome, which caused us to stop and think about what we could do differently. This is what keeps the problem-challenge carousel in motion. Spinning from one issue to the next, often with the same or similar strategies and tactics, and not getting our desired results. It's easy to think that the solution is to do more, to try harder, or to change tactics. But when focusing on "what can I do differently," you have just anchored yourself onto the carousel called Problem - Challenge. You enter a space of thinking about what you could do differently to get the desired results. In the journey of traditional success, you believe the problem exists in your outer world. You think about different systems, people, technology, tools, etc., that you could use to fix the problem, thereby getting your result. Your outer world is in control at this point.

The problem-challenge carousel is driven by the challenges of doing the right things to get the desired outcomes and fixing the stream of problems that come with unfulfilled outcomes and breakdowns. This carousel is a natural outgrowth of operating in the action-results domains. It is never-ending; the only thing that changes is the seat you are sitting on... but it is the same carousel.

But this outer focus misses the critical point.

Breakdowns arise from a misalignment within you, a disconnect in your observer. Problems and challenges are indicators, not of faulty actions, but of a disconnect between your authentic self and how you show up in the world. It's not about what you are doing wrong; rather, it is about who you are being that is generating these recurring problems and challenges. Until you recognize that the breakdown reflects the disharmony, think discordant energy, with your observer, you will remain trapped on the carousel, endlessly reacting to external circumstances without addressing the actual cause.

The exit sign to get off the carousel is within you, not on the carousel. The exit of the carousel exists in your observer domain. Your transformation to leap off this carousel occurs when you shift your perspective from doing, fixing problems, to understanding they exist as a reflection of who you are. Instead of reacting and asking what you can do differently, SOAR teaches you to reflect on who you are. Instead of viewing breakdowns as failures or setbacks, start to see them as opportunities for growth and to realign to your holistic success.

Look at yourself as the observer. Are you reacting from a scarcity, lack, frustration, and a fear-based mindset? If so, your ego, small self, is in control. You have shut the doors to your inner world, your true authentic self. If your egoic construct took over when reacting to the breakdown, you have "unplugged" yourself from your higher self. You hung up on your intuition. You have closed the doors on your imagination.

Stop and reflect. Listen to your soul, intuition, and imagination. Ask yourself if what you are doing is serving to fulfill your purpose? Is it aligned with the success you say you are committed to? Are you being past or future-focused?

Remember, your body, emotions, and language are a kaleidoscope! What are they showing you? What are they trying to tell you?

Note: When you feel frustrated, know you are acting in arrogance. Your ego has you, telling you that you should already know the answer to the issue, causing you to be frustrated. Observe your body, emotions, and language, as all three are coordinated with being frustrated. What is missing is being open and curious. Shifting your emotions to being open and curious transcends being frustrated, relaxes your body so you can think clearly, and your language and inner dialog shift to seeking solutions instead of focusing on why you did not get the desired result.

Reflecting on a problem or challenge in the context of who you are, as it relates to causing the problem, not what you are doing, opens you to new insights. New insights give you the power to transform and transcend the problem–challenge carousel. This is also where you lean into your courage and surrender.

Surrender to your higher self. Realizing your ego believes we must constantly be doing and fixing things to achieve happiness, peace, and success. Instead, connect to your soul observer with your intuition and imagination as your guides; this is what causes transformation in your life. Again, another perspective of realizing the problem is not "out there" but rather reflects an aspect of who you are, it is within you.

You can do the following things, grounded in your higher consciousness soul observer, to get and stay off the carousel. Yes, things to do. Notice and become aware of things, whether they keep you on the carousel or get you off it. Here are some contextual differences for you to reflect on.

Keeping you on: Ego
Exit off: Soul, intuition, and imagination.

Keeping you on: Doing, what can I do?"
Exit off: Being, "Who am I being?"

Keeping you on: Past focused
Exit off: Being future-focused.

Keeping you on: Focused on the outer world.
Exit off: Focused on your inner world.

Keeping you on: Context is a problem or challenge.
Exit off: Viewed as opportunities to grow and learn.
What is the lesson?

Keeping you on: Your inner conversations are "I'll try," "This is always difficult for me to do," "This might work."
Exit off: "I am committed to finding a resolution to this issue easily."

This is transformation in action. You're transforming your life instead of jumping onto another seat on the carousel. This is also building your "soul observer muscle."

Additionally, here are some things to do that will help and support you in continuing to build the strength of our soul observer and staying off the problem challenge carousel.

Be present. Stop. Breathe. Go within. Create your emotional state to one of openness, curiosity, and prosperity. Look for the lesson(s), gift(s), and opportunity(ies). This will allow you to recontextualize the problem or challenge, allowing you to see it differently, in ways you could not see a moment ago.

You as the observer. Observe yourself without judgment. Look for and at the emotions, beliefs, perspectives, and inner dialogue driving your actions. Are you acting from your ego and an "in order to" mindset? Are you locked into a belief system of how "it" must occur? What is your body trying to tell you? What beliefs do you hold about yourself that are causing, influencing, and driving your actions?

As your soul observer self, align yourself and connect yourself to your inner world. Your soul knows. Your intuition is the voice of the soul. Slow down. Reflect. Listen.

Reflection and Reframing. This ties into your observer self, another distinction for you to look into. From your soul observer self, reflect on the problem at hand as your higher self. Not just a casual reflection, but take time and be serious, not heavy, about how your past, culture, and history influence you. Is there an alignment with your soul, purpose, peace, and dignity?

When you can see the problem differently, you can reframe it. As you know from SOAR, you now have the power of your body, emotions, and language to help and support you in transforming and transcending yesterday's problem.

How can you see the problem or challenge by reflecting on it, looking to your past, and then shifting to being future-focused? In being future-focused and aligned with your life vision and purpose, what does your problem or challenge look like now? Or is it still a problem or challenge for you?

This or greater. Yes, you are committed to your desired results. Yes, you can now see and deal with the problem differently. But, just maybe, your soul has something greater in store for you. Be with your commitment to fulfilling your results commitments… without attachment. In doing so, you keep the doors open for something greater. Perhaps "this," whatever the problem is, was not supposed to work out because your soul is directing you on a different path. Because something bigger, better, and more in alignment with who you are, from a higher consciousness context, is waiting for you! Remember, it is not just about your success; it is about being holistically successful!

All of this serves to recontextualize your actions, to give you the ability to see things you couldn't before and the capacity to take actions you previously were unaware of.

Staying connected to your inner self as problems, more accurately said, your perceived problems arise, is your ticket to getting off the problem–challenge carousel. And staying off of it! You begin learning that life is less and less about fixing problems and dealing with challenges than evolving through them. Do you remember how to evolve in life? Love is spelled backwards in evolve. It is always about raising your consciousness. Always.

Let's look at two ways to learn to continue deepening your ability to transform your life, deal with breakdowns powerfully, and respond to them.

And it was Einstein who gave us the reason we need to stop and reflect in times of breakdowns to be able to transform that breakdown into an opportunity, always! To be able to transform, transcend, and heal (all that is applicable), the issue causing the breakdown prevents us from repeating it. Einstein's famous quote, "You cannot solve a problem with the same mind [consciousness] that created it." To say Einstein's quote differently, new knowledge and higher consciousness (which give new insights) are needed to approach breakdowns in a way that permanently resolves or transcends them. There are two ways to learn to do this: traditional learning and transformational learning.

Let's examine both from the perspective of a breakdown. You tried, and tried as you may, you did not fulfill your result commitment. Now what?

Traditional Learning

When you strive to achieve something, you are working towards fulfilling one of your results commitments. But anything can cause a breakdown, and with a breakdown, you're not fulfilling your result commitment.

The traditional success path has you immediately reacting and asking, "What can I do differently?" Or if you are collaborating with others, "What can we do differently?" This is the action domain's mantra in the traditional success model. You look for different people, different ways, different technology, and/or tools to achieve your desired result. You are convinced there is something, or someone, missing and that something different must occur; the occurring would then cause you to fulfill your goal (remember, goals are used in traditional success, results commitments are used in holistic success).

This approach is not wrong, as much good has come from this approach. Instead, I bring you the awareness (here is that word again!) of the traditional path to success and fulfilling your goals.

This path is known as traditional learning. It works at times, and it has merit. Traditional learning focuses on changing external actions, external circumstances, or something in your outer world, to achieve better outcomes.

194

This is you living your life between the results and action domains in SOAR.

Again, traditional learning has merit. But what happens when you can't obtain your results? What happens when you get your results, but the feelings of unfulfillment still linger or become overwhelming?

What happens when you try and fail? When your stress has you, and you can no longer think clearly? When do your results seem more like an impossibility than a reality? When does the effort needed to have your result begin to outweigh the benefits of its accomplishment?

This begs the question, "What is missing in traditional learning?"

You are!

The observer domain. Who is showing up to do the doing? The traditional success and learning model assumes the person or people showing up to do the doing have every element (reflect on the elements of your observer domain!) to get the desired result.

There is another domain of learning. It is called transformational learning.

Transformational Learning

Traditional learning, again, has its merits, but it also has its limitations. Stuck between the results and action domain, only so many fulfilled results commitments can come from this way of being, and then something has to change. And adding to this awareness is another rare and advanced skill. When things just aren't going well, declare a breakdown. Muddling in the stew of actions without being able to achieve your results, there comes a time when you say, "Enough is enough!" Declaring a breakdown is an act of self-empowerment.

This leads us into another fundamental element of SOAR: transformational learning. It is an exponentially powerful way to cause breakthroughs in your life and achieve results beyond your reach today, so much so that I suggest you bookmark this section for future reference.

Transformational learning is your "playbook" to your breakthrough. Let's begin in the same place we did with transformational learning, a breakdown. But now you will not jump on your habitual problem–challenge carousel and ask, "What am I going to do?" You are no longer focused on what different actions to take... at this point. Now, instead of oscillating between your results and action domain, you go back to your observer domain. By shifting to the observer domain, you have now put yourself at a new starting point to resolve your breakdown.

Let's explore how transformational learning is the key to unlocking your potential, giving you access to manifest any level of success you desire.

In the context of transformational learning, your breakdown is not a failure. It is an opportunity for deeper self-awareness and growth. There is no making wrong or blaming. To realize that the breakdown occurred most likely because of our habitual ways of being, thinking, and acting, which could not, or no longer, produce our desired outcome.

To move from the breakdown to a breakthrough, we have to move from reacting to observing, specifically, to be the soul observer. A powerful distinction of the soul observer is that it, or you, becomes the witness to the experience of a breakdown without judgment or attachment. This opens you to seeing the breakdown not as something happening *to* you but as something happening *for* you.

Feel your transformational shift!!

Now, we are going to observe the breakdown in two different ways. First, reflect on what caused or is causing your breakdown. Be hypervigilant not to drop into the action domain. Stay in your soul observer domain. Second, in the context of having already fulfilled your result commitment, who are you that is now causing this to happen?

As a reminder of our Learning and Competence section, which takes time and perseverance for the soul observer to "build its muscle" to do this.

Grounded and centered in your soul observer, let's lay out the blueprint to a breakthrough.

Begin by being open. Breathe. Take a moment to do whatever you need to let go of stress, frustration, or whatever emotion you need to release to be calm, centered, and grounded.

Begin with reflection, asking yourself probing and meaningful questions such as:

- What are your beliefs around this issue?

- Where do these beliefs come from?

- What does your culture tell you about why you are trying to achieve this result?

- What are others, teammates, colleagues, and cultural narratives telling you about how and why you should have this result?

- Who are you that has been trying to accomplish this goal?

- Did I catch you with this last question, "Who are you that has been trying to accomplish this goal?" Ego observer: Traditional success, as it is a goal. Soul observer: Holistic success, it would be a result commitment.

- What beliefs do your traditions hold that may be hindering you?

- Listen to your intuition! Your soul knows!

Operating in and attached to your egoic construct takes a lot of energy. When you shift, raise your consciousness, and connect to your soul, you connect to the flow of life. It is easy, with no effort required. Now you are open, and your openness is the only way divine wisdom, intuition, and imagination can reach you.

These are reflection points on the macro level. We have a lot more of your power for you to tap into. Bringing your body, emotions, and language into your breakdown will give you tremendous insights to be able to cause a breakthrough. Let's explore them separately to understand how they can help you cause a breakthrough, fulfill your result commitment, and give you greater success.

Beginning with your body. Your body is a profound teacher and is rarely viewed in this context. It holds somatic imprints of your emotional and energetic states. When you have a breakdown, the body reflects it through tightness, pain, or discomfort in specific areas. By turning your attention inward and scanning your body with curiosity and compassion, ask yourself, "Where am I holding this breakdown?" "What does this sensation have to tell me?" The sensations you are feeling are not random, rather they are messengers. They carry wisdom for you to be acknowledged, expressed, or released. Not doing this over an extended period of time will lead to a physical breakdown, dis-ease.

Remember, you are a spiritual being having a human experience, as your soul observer honors this, use your body as a partner to resolve your breakdown. The insights you gain from your body can point to the root cause of the breakdown, an unhealed wound, a limiting belief, or an unmet need. The breakdown may also have occurred because you ignored your boundaries or suppressed your truth. Your true authentic self has many ways to tell you that you are on the wrong path. Remember our prayer and affirmation, "And so it is, this or greater."

Your transformation happens when you honor the insights you gain from listening to your body. You then adjust your ways of being and integrate them into your daily life. Your body is a bridge between your soul observer, your inner wisdom, and your lived experience. You navigate in your body, moving from breakdown to breakthrough.

By becoming more consciously aware of your body's messages, you can respond to future problems and challenges with greater self-awareness and resilience.

Here are a few questions to reflect on to deepen your awareness of your body and uncover its wisdom.

- Be still and observe your breakdown from a place of stillness. What habits and recurring themes are you noticing that may have contributed to your breakdown?

- Scan your body with discernment. Where do you feel tension, discomfort, or a sensation? What would it tell you if that part of your body could speak to you?

- What emotions arise as you sit with your physical sensation that is connected to your breakdown? What message could this emotion be trying to tell you?

- In times of a breakdown, sit in your soul observer, without judgment. What deeper truth or insight comes to you about why this breakdown occurred? Feel and connect to your intuition and imagination.

- What might this breakdown show or ask you to let go of, embrace, or transform to create your breakthrough?

- Fully trusting the insights your body has shared with you, what is the next step you align with that causes your breakthrough, and you are willing to take right now?

Your reminder is to avoid thinking about doing something. Instead, stay connected to your divine wisdom and allow it to guide you into your action domain.

Next, we move to our emotional domain to cause transformational learning and our breakthrough. Let's continue.

Our emotions are rich beyond measure. They are our signals and gateways to profound and deep self-awareness and growth. Emotions do not happen randomly, they are messengers and give us lessons from our inner world, show us our needs, and deepen our understanding of the stories we tell ourselves. When it comes to a breakdown, our emotions may come with intensity, causing us to react to the circumstances, situations, events, or people. Emotions such as frustration, fear, resentment, or anger can spark our reactions. But rather than reacting in them, your transformational opportunity lies in *being with them as your soul observer.* The soul observer offers a space for higher energy emotions and is an extraordinarily sacred space.

When you allow yourself to observe your emotions, you can begin your inquiry into the wisdom, messages, and lessons they hold. You can ask yourself questions such as "What is this emotion showing me?" Anger, for example, reflects a perceived injustice. Sadness reflects something you care about deeply. Fear may stem from a lack of trust. Emotions are like roadmaps, each one pointing to your inner landscape. Instead of labeling them 'good' or 'bad,' transformational learning teaches you to see them as guideposts on your journey of self-awareness.

Your breakthrough happens when you stop resisting your emotions and instead allow them to flow through you and be informed by their wisdom. Lean into your emotions, witness them, feel them, and meet them with curiosity, compassion, and courage. Knowing that as your soul observer, doing this, you are always guided to your highest and best good. Allow your emotions to be an enlightening aspect of your evolution.

Here are a few questions to reflect on to gain deeper awareness of your emotions and uncover the wisdom they hold for you.

- In your reflection and silence, sitting with the dominant emotions of your breakdown, what may they be trying to tell you?

- Where in your body do you feel this emotion the strongest, and what happens when you simply observe it? Don't try to change or do anything with it, simply observe it.

- If your emotion had a voice, what would it want to tell you now? What is the message it wants you to hear?

- What story from your past are you telling yourself about this emotion? Is your holding you back or serving your growth?

- What might this emotion be protecting you from feeling or facing on a deeper level? You may want to ask yourself this question three to five times to get to the root cause of the initial emotion.

- Imagine fully releasing from this emotion, what shift is possible? What would be your next step to anchor your new awareness?

You are evolving! Having these deeper conversations with your body and emotions opens you to new knowledge and insights. You know the power of new knowledge and insights! And we are not complete with our transformative inquiry to cause your breakthrough.

Are you staying out of your habit of wanting to do something and staying centered in your soul observer?

Body, emotions, and now let's embark in the world of language.

Language is a creative force unto itself. Listening to others and yourself describe the situations and events surrounding and giving the breakdown, you can see the all but guaranteed future that has been created. It is that obvious once you become aware of it.

It is our inner dialogue you especially want to focus on in a breakdown. Most people default to descriptive language, telling stories, trying to figure out who or what is to blame, and how they feel trapped, a.k.a., are victims. While descriptive language plays a role in your breakthrough and is necessary to bring clarity to what is so, we must shift into generative language to cause new results.

As your soul observer, you are aligned with your inner world by using generative language and being true to your authentic self. From a place of higher consciousness, the soul observer can see patterns of language that created the breakdown and can create the breakthrough. It is also noticing the place you where or are speaking from. Are you speaking from a place of powerlessness or empowerment? From limitation of inevitability? Are you using words or phrases open to creating possibilities, inviting curiosity, and creating new pathways forward? Or is your language stuck in habitual patterns of your past... and you are trying to get new results?

Phrases like "I knew this was going to happen" or "This always happens to me," solidifies the outcome. These, and similar beliefs, focus on lack and not having. As you give you get. What you focus on the universe provides.

Transformational learning and generative language see the breakdown as opportunities for growth. And you operate knowing that nothing is happening *to* you. This is a great time to remind yourself of how integrity plays a role in breakthroughs to occur. Shift your inquiry in generative language to "What is this breakdown teaching me?" or "How can I grow from this experience?" Now you are unlocking new emotional and physical responses as words that don't just describe, they define your state of being.

As you now know, your body, emotions, and language are both a kaleidoscope and bridges. Being able to speak your emotions and body sensations into existence is using your language as a bridge between your inner and outer worlds.

Here are a few questions to reflect on to gain deeper awareness of your language and uncover the wisdom it holds for you.

- When describing your current breakdown to yourself or others, what recurring words or phrases do you notice? Are they limiting or empowering?

- As your soul observer, rewrite the story of your breakdown. What words, feelings, and emotions do you evoke and express through your language? How do you tell the story differently?

- What declarations can you make to yourself to cause a breakthrough?

- How do you speak about your emotions and body sensations? Are you allowing them to express themselves clearly and with compassion?

- When you share your breakdown with others, are you doing it from an energy of separation and blame or of collaboration and connection?

- What one word or phrase can you choose, and hold, that causes and guides you in transforming your breakdown into a breakthrough? To be resolute is one example.

It is generative language that creates your reality. Language is both a portal and a mirror. The Laws of Attraction and Cause and Effect are always working, and whether you use them to limit yourself or create your life, the choice is always yours.

Knowing the power of yourself as your soul observer, reflecting on your breakdown, using your body, emotions, and language to deal, heal, and transcend a breakdown is life-altering. How you deal with breakdowns is now forever changed. Instead of fearing conflict and breakdowns, you know they are an opportunity to grow and evolve. You also hold the rare and advanced skill of learning to declare a breakdown is self-empowering and causes transformation in your life. Transformation to cause you to get new results.

Transformational learning is another element of SOAR to allow you to be able to see what you can't see today. To acquire new knowledge and gain new insights. This gives you the ability to act in ways you can't today. You're gaining new capabilities and capacities... you're evolving. This speaks to the holistic aspect of transformational learning and, in part, is how Jack Mezirow (the Godfather of transformational learning) defines it. Mezirow "...suggested that transformational learning has not occurred until an individual has acted on the learning."

Feel the difference between habitually going from the results domain to the action domain, and instead, going from the results domain to the observer domain.

Feel the difference between traditional and transformational learning. They are worlds apart!

Changing the course of your life from traditional to transformational learning puts you on a new path to manifesting your holistic success. To overcome limitations and struggles of the past and chart a future where you are the architect of it.

Manifesting Your Success

Gaining new knowledge through transformational learning leads to the ability to take new actions. You are now approaching your actions not only with new knowledge but also with new insights gained from your transformational learning journey. Plus, you are taking your new learning and applying it, being future-focused.

And you take the actions you do to manifest your success. Manifestation is not simply about wishing for something to appear in your life. Rather, it is about you, as your soul observer self, *embodying* your desired results *from a place, in the energy, of having already fulfilled your desired results.* It is *not* about manifesting to get something, but manifesting from already having something. This subtle but profound distinction is the key to unlocking true manifestation.

This is another way to say that your observer self, results commitments, and success are *all in energetic alignment before you take one action.*

When they try to manifest financial abundance, better health, a relationship, or a better career, most people do so from a place of lack. They think, "I want this because I don't have it." This inadvertently strengthens the very state they are trying to escape: the state of *not having*. What you resist persists. What you focus on magnifies. Wanting and not having are states also.

The universe responds to our very essence, our level of consciousness, our frequency. This is again why you, your soul observer self, are the heart, literally, of your holistic success.

Your desires fail to manifest into your reality because you essentially say, "I want this because I do not yet have it." You just created a trap for yourself by wanting instead of one who has. Our desire for acquisition confirms and perpetuates our state, our level of consciousness, of *not having.* Paradoxically, the more we chase after something, the more we affirm its absence in our lives. And as we affirm lack, we receive more lack. The universe is giving us what we are aligned with. With our vibration of lack, the universe supports our lack vibration... no matter how desperately we desire something different.

Your secret to manifesting your success lies in a radical shift in perspective. Rather than desiring from a state of not having, again, you must embody the state of already having. Where we energetically align ourselves with our soul observer, and with our results commitments as though they are already real. Who you are is one who already has what is desired. There is no more powerful place or way to manifest than this.

Aligning yourself to your results commitments as though they are already fulfilled and real, alters your thoughts, feelings, beliefs, body, emotions, and language. You shift from the lower energy of lack to the higher vibrations of your success!

Regardless of your outer world today, how do you embody the state of fulfillment and your success when nothing in your outer world reflects it? Here are some practical steps to shift your consciousness from wanting to having:

- **Identity Redefinition:** This is where transformational learning becomes exponentially powerful because it gives you knowledge and insights to redefine your identity, who you are. You redefine yourself not as someone pursuing a result but as someone who already embodies it.

- **Act as If:** This does not mean spending beyond your means or pretending. Instead, it means acting as though you are already aligned with the frequency to which you are committed. This is where your imagination, which you call Christ consciousness or your soul, becomes your lifeline. How would someone act, think, feel, and interact? Aligning your actions with your desired results commitments creates a loop: "as you give, you receive," reinforcing your new levels of consciousness.

- **Shift from Desire to Gratitude:** If you desire something, start by practicing gratitude for "it" as if it is already present. Gratitude reorients us to abundance and prosperity, reminding us of all we have. Gratitude expands your perception of connection... connection to your results commitment already being fulfilled.

- **Visualize as a Completed State:** Rather than visualizing your results commitments as a distant future, visualize them as your current reality. This shift in your perception influences your subconscious and trains you to recognize the feeling of having rather than wanting. Additionally, the only place you can manifest anything is in the present. Always in the present but future-focused! If you visualize your result commitment as having it next week, or next year, any time in the future, you are guaranteed to keep it in your future and never realize it.

- **Detach from the Outcome.** Authentic manifestation does not mean obsessing over a specific outcome: it is about allowing the universe to unfold in alignment with your state of consciousness. When we let go of attachment to a specific outcome, we allow our highest good to manifest. Your soul knows, your ego may still be offering up its limitations. A prayer to offer in your manifestation is "And so it is, this or greater." And so it is, is a declaration. This or greater is saying to the universe, "I am open to receive, this or greater. I am open to my highest good, my highest calling." This is an opportunity to build your faith, knowing your higher self is always taking care of you.

When we embody the consciousness of already having fulfilled our results commitments, we no longer act as beggars of the universe. Instead, we become co-creators, which is acting in alignment with our true authentic self. This is why manifestation is an "inside out" process, creating your observer self to be successful and allowing the universe to support your journey.

Remember, manifestation is not about begging or bending the universe to your way or will. If you feel this, know your ego, your small self, is in control. Instead, as your divine self, your infinite creator self, it is about aligning with the flow of the universe that is always abundant. When you embody the experience of already having, you open yourself to receiving not as a seeker but as an aligned being. True manifestation flows not from striving but from residing in the truth of who you are: a spiritual being having a human experience, a divine creator.

And an extraordinarily powerful system to transform your life, while keeping the seductive old habit patterns in your past where they belong, is to create a life vision for your new, future, authentic, true, and inspiring life. A life vision is your future successful life that you author! Couple your life vision with SOAR, and you can move mountains to do and have anything you want in your life. Where you literally are the architect of your destiny, divine creator!

Life Vision to Mastery

Imagine your life where every decision you make, every action you take, is purposefully taken. They are in conscious *response* to the circumstances in your life. Circumstances that you create. And most importantly, every step and action is a deliberate step toward your future that you have consciously and deliberately created.

This is the power of a life vision.

Life Vision to Mastery is a program offered through the OM Spiritual Center. It incorporates the teachings of SOAR into a highly personalized life vision. Consistent with all the teachings of the OM Spiritual Center, it is grounded in the philosophies of ontology and metaphysics. Imagine the transformative power of a life vision that you create, design, build, and live into that is built on the ancient wisdom and universal principles of these philosophies!

Life Vision to Mastery teaches you how to design a life vision that is a personalized blueprint for your life that *you author*, create, and design in six domains of your life. It takes your hopes and dreams and turns them into a future-focused plan that anchors you in a life of purpose and fulfillment. Being future-focused unlocks your potential, and you live your life with purpose, focus, direction, clarity, and velocity. It is how you transcend the problems and challenges that once seemed insurmountable. It is how you rise above the cacophony of your past, your history, your culture, the unconscious limiting patterns that have silently shaped your life, and take control of your destiny. Having a life vision is how you become the architect of your destiny!

Life Vision to Mastery gives you the knowledge and empowers you to stop being a passive participant in your life and become the author, architect, and creator of your life. While your life vision is meticulously designed, it is flexible and evolves with you.

Now imagine... learning SOAR, a transformational blueprint, with a multidisciplinary and holistic approach to life. SOAR is a fundamental foundation for your success. Now, couple this with the *Life Vision to Mastery* program, your *personalized* life vision blueprint for your success!

This combination alters your life to your soul!

You begin by creating your life vision from nothing, no-thing. No-thing, is where everything is possible. You free yourself from the constraints and limitations of your past. Today's constraints and limitations, which give you the problems and challenges you face today, come from your past. They can only exist in your life vision if you take them from your past and put them in your life vision!

This is a contextual shift in how you live your life. This is how you turn possibilities and dreams into reality. Your focus is not primarily on what you are doing or going to do, but rather on *who you are and who you are becoming.*

Imagine your life when your past no longer dictates your future. Your historical and cultural narratives that once held you back are replaced by self-empowering declarations you crafted. Declarations that create your future reflect the highest expression of who you are and what you desire to achieve at your soul level.

This is living your life with power, intention, and most importantly, being authentic to yourself. Life now becomes about authoring your own story, free of your past. Again, bring anything you want from your past, history, and culture into your life vision, but I think you can already see that, to the extent you do, you have recontextualized its meaning. Whatever you bring from your history and culture into your life vision now serves you; you no longer are serving them. Being aligned with your true authentic self infuses your life with purpose, imagination, and intention, living your life on a path that brings you fulfillment.

A life vision anchors you operating in your life with a forward vision. You unlock and live into your potential!

Breathe.

Pause.

Feel the transformational difference between traditional and holistic success, and what new possibilities you can already see with a life vision supporting you!

A life vision is created from you being your soul observer. You are connected to the spirit of your success. Again, this is success that you author what success is and means to you. And you create this in six areas of your life.

This is what causes you to alter your perspectives and perceptions of life. This gives you access to knowledge and insights you did not know or see a moment ago. You simply were not aware. Creating your life vision in conjunction with the knowledge you gain from learning SOAR will put your life into a new world!

Yes, it is that powerful.

Yes, it is that transformational.

Note: For more information and to create your Life Vision to Mastery, visit **omspiritualcenter.com/life-vision-to-mastery**

Bringing and sustaining success in your life with purpose, focus, clarity, direction, and, to the level you want to turn it up, velocity, requires creating, designing, constantly editing, and living from your life vision. *Life Vision to Mastery* teaches you how to create your life vision in six domains. You author your future-focused life vision in these domains:

1. Spiritual
2. Physical Well-being
3. Personal
4. Financial
5. Professional / Retirement
6. Relationships

These six domains are what ensure you live in harmony in your life. You no longer, for example, are hell-bent on the traditional success model in your profession at the expense of the other domains of your life.

The order in which you create these domains in your Life Vision to Mastery is intentional. The first three are about you. The first three domains of your life vision have you consciously and holistically create your life. Then, you anchor this holistic way of being into your life until you embody it: it is who you are and who you are becoming.

I call this being altruistically selfish. Before you can be of service to others, you have to take care of yourself first.

Your spiritual domain in your life vision is first. We are spiritual beings having a human experience, not a human being with a soul. This is creating and designing your life from the essence of who you are. As Socrates said many years ago, "Know thyself." You consciously connect to your essence, your soul, to know thyself. With this connection, you now define who you are and who you are becoming. By connecting to your intuition and imagination, your heart's wisdom, you live your life connected to your soul and connected to what gives you joy, peace, prosperity, purpose, and fulfillment. This creates a foundation for your life that transcends the outer world and the pressures and expectations of your history and culture. Creating your spiritual domain in your life vision causes you to live your life being authentic to your true self.

Humans' physical bodies carry them through life. Optimizing health to fulfill one's life vision is second to our spiritual life vision domain. Without good physical health, we cannot fulfill the rest of our life vision. When asked what surprised him most about humanity, the Dalai Lama answered, "Man. Because he sacrifices his health in order to make money. Then he sacrifices his money to recuperate his health."

A reflection point for you. Reflect on these first two domains of a life vision, and their order. How well do you "know thyself?" Do you take care of your body in the context of it being a vehicle to give your soul the experience of having a human experience? Do you feel the purposeful order and connection of these two domains? How would your life be different if you lived in this knowing?

Rounding out the first three domains of your life vision is the personal domain of your life vision. This, in part, is a "catch-all" in that if something does not fit in the other domains of your life vision, you put it in your personal section. This is where you define all the other elements that constitute your personal life that are not included in the other five life vision domains.

Aligning with a fundamental aspect of SOAR, I highly encourage you to make lifelong learning and personal development a high priority in your personal life vision. To embark on the infinite journey to "know thyself," to evolve to your Self. This, again, is the journey of evolving and self-mastery. I invite you to take a moment and note anything that comes to mind for you in this area.

What else comes to mind for you in a broader spectrum of your personal domain? Maybe there is a creative side of you that has been suppressed for years... decades, which is longing to express? Defining and setting boundaries in your work-life balance is defined in your personal life vision. This is the domain that, as the name implies, is the most personalized part of your life vision.

Again, the first three domains, and their order, are very intentional. When you "know thyself," the rest of your life falls into place. Having these first three domains defined, anchored, embodied, and most importantly, being in energetic alignment with all of them, allows you to stay focused, have direction, be in your life with clarity, and to be able to act with velocity on your holistic success journey.

These are also the beginning of creating your future life and *responding into life*. Responding into life and intentionally being future-focused. This also gives you the awareness not to be sucked into the seduction of the drama, uncertainties, fear, and change (for the sake of change) of today's uncertain world. Now you transcend the cacophony of the outer world, tuned into only what matters most to you.

Be true to your authentic self.

Be altruistically selfish.

You will no longer react to things, circumstances, situations, events, and people on a short-term, sensational, and emotional basis. Instead, you will respond to them with higher emotions and in higher states of consciousness. In these higher states of consciousness, you will act to fulfill your life vision, experiencing holistic success.

Moving onto the fourth domain in your life vision, financial, you create your financial life vision domain before your professional domain. Again, this is intentional. In creating your first three life vision domains, you define and author your future self. You define who you are and who you are becoming. The fourth domain is your leap to the outside world from your inner world.

Having the financial domain before the professional domain also serves a larger purpose: fulfilling one's *life vision.*

Acting in the wholeness of your life vision, it takes money to fulfill your purpose and your life vision. Putting your financial life vision before your professional life vision is transformational. It ensures your career will align with your true authentic self and ensure your income from your career will fulfill your financial life vision.

A transformational insight SOAR offers you in creating holistic success is that your financial and professional life visions reflect who you are. They no longer define you, which is what traditional success does.

Now you define what you want for yourself financially. When you create your professional life vision, you will be creating it from having clarity about who you are, the first three domains of your life vision. Additionally, you have defined financial clarity for yourself. Who are you, and how much money are you committed to making before creating your professional domain? Do you see... and *feel...* this paradigm shift?!

This can literally be a life-altering awareness.

A note of caution. I have witnessed this countless times, when someone has the "million-dollar idea" and cannot buy me a cup of coffee because they do not have the funds. People define themselves by the *possibility* of their future without anchoring within themselves what it takes for it to happen. This is a dream, not a future reality.

Do not confuse hobbies and wishes with your profession.

That is not to say you do not have the next billion-dollar business or a revolution in some business sector, but if you are not making a living from it, it is currently a hobby at best. SOAR teaches you how to turn any dream or wish into reality... just be mindful of old habits and your inner dialogue holding you back vs. empowering yourself with the teachings of SOAR to make it happen.

Also, if you don't have or create your financial foundation today, your retirement years may be more of a nightmare than living your dreams.

Figuring out and defining your financial objectives brings focus, clarity, direction, and velocity to your professional domain. It gives deeper purpose to your inspiration. You now act with certainty fueled by your inner wisdom. Your actions are for your long-term life fulfillment, and you are not tempted by short-term pleasures. This is a huge component to creating lasting success in your life and new levels of holistic success.

Creating your financial life vision before your professional life vision may even cause you to rethink your professional and retirement domains!

Having a conversation about your financial life vision, including why it is in front of your professional / retirement life vision, is one of the most mature conversations you can have with yourself (and spouse/partner)!

I invite you to pause and reflect on these four life vision domains. Feel the transformative power of the *Life Vision to Mastery* program. Imagine authoring your future success regardless of your past or current circumstances. Reflect on the teachings that SOAR has shared with you up to this point.

How much harmony and prosperity are you experiencing in your life today?

How much holistic success are you experiencing in your life today?

Reflect on who you are instead of what you are doing and experiencing.

How well do you truly know yourself, and honor your true authentic self in your profession?

Remember, it is not about being right or wrong but about self-awareness, the beginning of all transformation.

Notice, again, that the first three domains in your life vision are before how much money you will make and what you will do: your profession. You can have as much prosperity as you want, but SOAR is about a contextual shift in your finances and profession. Your finances and profession no longer define you; they reflect who you are.

Let me share a story that I have known about for over 40 years. In fairness, The Social Security The Administration does not say when it was published or updated, but it serves to make my point, and I trust that the numbers have not altered that much over the last forty-plus years. One fact that makes me believe these numbers have not changed that much is that current statistics show 40% of retired people in the U.S. have Social Security as their sole source of income. Also, it was designed to be 40% of your retirement income.

I offer the *Social Security Administration's 100 Man Story* to further the importance of why you create your financial life vision before you create your professional life vision. Simply put, numbers do not lie.

With over 30 years of mortgage banking experience, I have experienced this story many times. I have worked with many clients from a wide range of socioeconomic backgrounds. In the last several years, I have exclusively worked with reverse mortgages, so my clients are at least 62. My clientele gives me real-life insight into the accuracy of these figures.

The 100 Man Story

Take any group of 100 people starting their careers and follow them for 40 years until they reach retirement age, and here is what you will find:

- Only 1 will be wealthy.
- 4 will be financially secure.
- 5 will continue to work, not because they want to, but because they have to.
- 36 will be dead.
- 54 will be dead broke.

That is...

5% successful
95% unsuccessful,
90% dead or dead broke.

Again, numbers do not lie.

SOAR serves as a fundamental foundation for altering who you are and, in part, how you relate to your finances. Enrolling in the *Life Vision to Mastery* program and coupling it with the teachings of SOAR all but guarantees you will not be part of the 54% club.

Figuring out and defining your financial results commitments, and then "backing into" your profession, will give you a wake-up call or peace of mind. You will know whether your profession will fulfill your financial life vision and secure your golden years, your retirement.

By creating and clarifying your financial commitments in your financial life vision, you are ensuring your financial security. It also gives you the freedom to make choices that align with your true authentic self and have holistic success. Now your profession is in service to fulfill your financial commitments. This is a transformative moment, as traditional success says make the money, go for power, and fame. Holistic success and your life vision make your finances and professional life a reflection of your inner self, again with your profession in service to fulfill your financial life vision.

With the first three domains of your life vision and your financial life vision created, which aligns with your first three life vision domains, it is time to create your professional life vision. Allow your inner wisdom to guide you on this journey, unplugging from the societal norms and cultural narratives that have been influencing you. A key question is "Why do you want the profession you do?" Remember, your profession is now an out picturing of your inner world. Feel it, your soul knows. You may keep your current profession... great. You may strive to grow in your current profession... great. You may leave the job and embark on a new venture (do this responsibly!) ...

great. Whatever you are guided to do, you are now doing it guided by your inner wisdom. This is a recontextualization of your professional life.

This alignment of the first five of your life vision domains allows you to create holistic success, which is lasting success. Are you feeling the lights of illumination shining on your path of self-mastery? Is your path becoming clearer? Are you feeling unsettled at one level, yet there is a deep resonance of truth speaking to you?

Completing this highlight of the *Life Vision to Mastery* program is the relationship domain of your life vision. Your relationship life vision is to consciously define who you want relationships with and how you want those relationships to be. And how you want them to be isn't about controlling the relationship; rather, it is about the energy you bring to the relationship. It is from the energy you create, as your soul observer, that you bring into the relationship.

Once you establish your energy for a relationship, you define what things and actions you are committed to in the relationship. A classic example is creating a date night with your spouse or partner. As a grandfather, may I suggest that there may be certain things you want to do with your grandchildren? In your relationship domain, you also define family and friends that matter to you. What do those relationships look like? If there are special relationships with colleagues that you want to include in your relationship domain, please do.

Your relationship's life vision also includes people, whether they are still in this dimension or not, with whom you are or have had a breakdown. If you have someone who has passed away and there was a broken relationship at the time of death, you bring that relationship into your life vision to heal and transform.

A personal and deeply touching story I will share with you concerning broken relationships. My daughter and I had a breakdown and had hardly spoken for a couple of years. I put this into my life vision, defined the relationship I was committed to, energetically created it, and saw her, unplanned, within a month of creating this part of my life vision. Within a minute, quite literally, the healing happened, and to this day, we have a great relationship, and I cannot imagine anything different.

We are all One, expressing uniquely in our human experience. I suggest you create a conclusion paragraph for your relationship domain. Define who you are in relation to all others, both human and natural. Being open, compassionate, understanding, humble, and loving are all great emotions that can help you define this.

SOAR is your fundamental foundation for life. *Life Vision to Mastery* is your personal fundamental foundation for life. These are two master blueprints that allow you to author your future life, regardless of what your past has held.

This is holistic success.

This is evolving.

This is self-mastery.

Making SOAR a Reality in Your Life

In pursuing success, it is essential to recognize that your success is determined by the internal dynamics of who you are, your level of consciousness, and whether it is your ego or soul that you are allowing to control your life. This is what determines how you perceive the world and the conscious choices you make. As your observer self, you define your thoughts, beliefs, body, emotions, language, behaviors, actions, perceptions, the results you achieve, and the level of success you attain.

SOAR is a lifelong experiential journey. It is an infinite journey within, creating, designing, editing, and living into your future, a future free of your past limiting challenges and beliefs that your culture and history gave you, and you now choose to release. A future that you create from your heart's wisdom and intuition. This is done by taking on learning SOAR, as it is a lifelong journey of learning and the practical application of its principles, strategies, and knowledge. This is how you create, design, and live as your true authentic self.

Where to begin on your journey?

You begin exactly where you are.

We all step out of ignorance in our desire for something better and begin our journey as beginners. On your lifelong learning journey, you practice and get a coach or teacher to ensure you practice the right things. Your life vision helps you stay on course and align with your purpose. This is the path and your lifelong journey to self-mastery.

To make SOAR a reality in your life, I offer the following advice to help and support you in creating and sustaining new and higher levels of success.

SOAR: Take on learning SOAR to the level of mastery, you embody it. Continuously create and look for ways to apply the teachings of SOAR to your life. Personalize SOAR. It holds all the components to create and have any level of success you desire; the rest is up to you.

Life Vision to Mastery program: Create your life vision to personalize the teachings of SOAR. A life vision as your personalized blueprint, in real time, always available to edit as your life shows up, for your holistic success. It defines your success in all the critical areas of your life. It incorporates the body, emotions, language, strategies, and tactics to live your life by design, purposefully, and to have a fulfilling life. This is your personalized blueprint to creating and living into your holistically successful life. While always living in the present and being future-focused, it is your life vision that creates your future; you are now the architect of your future.

Self-Awareness: Nothing happens without awareness. To bring the unconscious conscious is the first step in any change and transformation in your life. Cultivate a deep understanding of your thoughts, beliefs, emotions, language, and behaviors. These hold the wisdom and the lessons to augment your transformational journey of success. Recognize patterns rooted in the ego and work towards aligning them with your higher self, your soul. Remember, fear or love? Separation or Oneness? Struggle or peace? Connect with your inner voice. It holds the wisdom you are looking for.

Reflection: Practice hitting the pause button in your life. Schedule downtime to be with yourself. To contemplate and reflect on who you are. Why are you doing the things you are doing in your life? Why do you have the relationships you have in your life? What are your passions in life? What is your soul wanting to tell you? What inspires you? What is your body trying to say to you? Scheduling downtime for yourself in a world where we have an "I don't have time" crisis is a priceless investment in yourself. You may gain insights in your downtime that would never be revealed if you kept running at the pace of our egoic world. Although reflecting is looking back on your past, this is not to be underestimated in its ability to give you insights and knowledge to transform your life and life into a future that may be beyond your dreams today. Also, remember your life now is about manifesting your holistic success. So, take time to create a practice of reflecting in all six areas of your life vision to gain deeper insight and authentic awareness of yourself. Reflection coupled with transformational learning is yet another recipe to be able to move mountains.

I want to offer you a journaling exercise to help you reflect on any issue you are stuck in or that is confronting you. First, form a question about a problem in an area you are stuck, challenged, struggling with, or flat out having a breakdown in. It can be in any domain, area, or anything you want to address in your life. You can use this exercise anytime and with anyone or anything you struggle with.

I also strongly recommend pen and paper for this journaling exercise. By physically writing, you engage parts of your brain that you do not if you use a keyboard.

Do you have a question? Do not continue until you do.

Now, the journaling assignment. Write the question. Immediately write the answer that comes to you... Do not think about it, write! Now, *the constant in this exercise is that you do NOT change the question!*

Write the question again. Write the answer, the first thing that comes to you. Again, write, do not think.

Your pen should not stop between writing the question and writing the answer.

Do this at least 10 - 12 times: same question, write the first thing that comes to you. You will feel when you have gone through your superficial, getting-by, dismissive, B.S. answers. You may experience answering a few questions and feeling stuck and/or frustrated. KEEP WRITING! Then, you will feel yourself connect with your essence and your heart's wisdom. You may also experience your intuition talking to you. Whether your written word, your intuition, or a combination, your soul knows the answer. And the answer from your true authentic self will come. You will feel and know it. You will write yourself through the limitations of your egoic construct and connect with your heart's wisdom.

Desire: Having awareness is the seed of anything happening in your life. Desire is rooted in knowing and wanting to live purposefully and have a fulfilling life. Be extremely mindful of your self-talk here, as many times people brush off their soul's desire as a wish or dream, not realizing that it is their future reality they are saying no to. Connect with your intuition and your imagination. As is said, you would not have insight, dreams, or desires unless you are capable of fulfilling them. Caution comes with desire. Desire is void of action. Lean into and honor your desires. Be conscious of whether what you think is a desire is really wishful thinking. It is your reaction to something in your outer world. It might be a moment of daydreaming and not an authentic desire. Once you have defined an authentic desire, utilize the knowledge SOAR shares to turn your desires into reality.

Knowledge: It takes new knowledge to get new results. As simple as this sounds, it requires you to be open, curious, wonder, and be a beginner (despite years of education or experience). It is what we, what humanity does not know, that is our biggest area of knowledge. So, we still have much to learn. To have the courage to put the past aside and be open to learning. It takes our superpower of humility to be open to new knowledge. Hubris is what keeps the gates to new knowledge locked. Hubris and ignorance guarantee that holistic success will always be out of reach for you. Courage and humility are extraordinarily powerful when using transformational learning to gain new knowledge.

Insights: It also takes new insights to get new results. Knowledge and insights are like first cousins. But knowledge is objective, external, and exists whether we are aware of it or not. Insights are subjective, internal, happen outside of time, and are generative. The access to insights comes from both our level of consciousness and from reflection, questioning, and having new awareness. It is again our friend humility that opens you to having insights. Insights are your communication with the divine. Honor their wisdom.

Purpose: We have a crisis in our world today. The crisis is because people lack purpose. Genuine, authentic, rooted in your soul, purpose. Combining self-awareness, reflection, desire, journaling, and prayer can lead you to your authentic purpose in life. Your soul knows you came into this lifetime with a purpose, talents, and gifts. Your journey of their discovery is priceless and life-altering.

Language: Pay attention, be mindful, to the words you use, both externally and your internal self-talk. In fact, pay critical attention to your inner dialogue. Your outer world, what you want, and your success are but a reflection of your inner dialogue. Words create. Create your life, declare a new you, a new future, beginning with your words. Eliminate words and phrases such as I'll try, I wish, I will, I might, maybe, I should, or I hope so. These are all affirmations of your failure to achieve your desired success. Instead, declare your life into existence. Use language to declare, define, and affirm your success. Use generative language to create your life and future, regardless of your past. Language holds frequencies. Align your body, emotions, and language in the same frequency before taking action. Remember the kaleidoscope metaphor of your body, emotions, and language.

Emotional Intelligence: Emotions, energy - in - motion. They come with messages and lessons. Take on emotions as teachers; there is much to learn from them. We are taught to ignore, suppress, and deny our emotions. SOAR offers you two critical distinctions in the emotional domain. First, as your observer and divine creator, you can create your emotions and moods in any circumstance, situation, event, *and with any person.* Second, when you consciously create your emotion, you *respond* into life holding that emotion. This transcends reacting and keeps you anchored to your essence. These are rare and advanced skills. This is the critical distinction and complete opposition to the path of traditional success, where you mostly ignore your emotions and react in the emotion as they come up. Be especially mindful of *reacting* in your ego or *responding* from your soul. They are worlds apart!

Connect with Your Virtues: Journaling is an excellent practice for becoming aware of your virtues. What matters most to you? What are your strong virtues? What do you care most about? Be authentic, honor yourself regardless of what your culture or history suggests to you. Your virtues are one of your cornerstones to creating your life vision.

Care: Life gives us a lot to be concerned about. Some are long-term, others are for a reason or a season. But we only act on the concerns that we care about. What do you care about most in your life? In the six domains of your life vision, what do you care about most in each domain? Become present to what you care about most in your life. Care and your purpose in life are interconnected. Your purpose is what you care about most in your life.

Body Awareness: Tune into your body's signals. Physical sensations can be indicators of alignment or misalignment with your true self. Pay attention to your body as you go through your day. It is the vehicle you experience this lifetime with, so honor it, and it will help and support you in the other areas of your life. Couple your emotional awareness with your body awareness. Reminder, emotions, suppressed, repressed, denied, or ignored, express themselves physically with time. Listening to your body will tell you where you have suppressed an emotion. Listening to your body, asking it a question, and listening to its wisdom. I was once asked in a coaching session what my little finger would have to say about the issue the coach and I were discussing. I received a very insightful answer!

Intuition Development: Your soul is calling. Everyone experiences intuition. It is at the essence of who you are. Trust your instincts, they never lie. Cultivate a connection with your intuitive wisdom, also known as your heart's wisdom. Your brain was meant to be the servant to your heart's wisdom. The world today lives mostly backwards to our truth, believing the brain and logic are what should be our guiding forces. It is time to take back your power from the ignorant beliefs given to us from the Scientific Revolution in the 17th century.

Practice. Practice. Practice. In a world where we strive to do more, to do better... and faster, we often think we should be a pro when we step on the court. It simply does not work that way in life. It takes practice. Experiencing frustration here is one of our enemies of learning. Frustration is our ego talking and is a form of arrogance. It also takes practicing the right things to be a master of your life. And it takes time. Be patient with yourself and maintain your focus, clarity, and direction in pursuing the fulfillment of your life vision and being holistically successful.

Breakdowns: They are part of life. Taking responsibility for the fact that you are experiencing a breakdown gives you access to being in the present and creating a breakthrough for yourself. Breakdowns and breakthroughs occur in language. But like a kaleidoscope, your emotions and your body are tied to how your language occurs. You also, instinctively, will know how and when to persevere and have determination by learning the SOAR model. Another advanced observer skill is knowing how and when to declare a breakdown in your life to cause a breakthrough. Knowing how and when to do this is an element of self-mastery.

Be Present: You cannot change the past, but you can, in moments of reflection, learn from it. Worry and anxiety all but guarantee you will not obtain the success to which you are committed. The reason you will not attain success with worry and anxiety is that your focus is on what you say you do not want. Worry and anxiety are both emotions that take you out of the present. Remember, too, the Laws of Attraction and Cause and Effect are always working!

The only reality we have is the infinite now, the present. This is where your power to create your life is. Your transformative power of being in the present is also consciously being aware of the direction in which you live your life.

Is your life built on your past, things you do not like, don't want, limitations, problems, challenges, struggles, and breakdowns inherent in your history and culture? If this is your focus, you have "filed" what you do not want in your future and locked in your almost certain future given by your past. This is not the future. This is reliving your past over, and over, and over, thinking you are living into a new future. Your reality is more like the tennis ball going back and forth in a tennis game. You are bouncing back and forth between your past and your future, reliving your past, and you are never present.

As you have learned with SOAR, being your soul observer means being grounded and centered in the present and future-focused. In your self-empowerment, this means authoring and living into a future you create, regardless of your past.

Making SOAR a reality is learning and embodying its strategies and tactics. This is a journey of acquiring new knowledge and gaining new insights to create, design, and live the life of your dreams, to have holistic success in your life, regardless of your past.

As your soul observer and author of your SOARing success, make SOAR your own. Please feel free to add anything that helps and supports you in embodying the SOAR model and making SOAR a reality in your life. Remember, it is experiential; it is meant to be lived!

Integrating these practices into your daily life creates an experiential model for success beyond external achievements. Connected to and aligning with your essence, you will know your purpose, declare your results commitments into your life, and SOAR to levels of success that perhaps yesterday, you couldn't have dreamed of what is possible.

With SOAR, your holistic success is a transformative and lifelong journey with purpose and fulfillment.

Your journey of evolving.

Your journey to self-mastery.

Blessings on your journey of transforming your human experience.

Your Next Steps

First, congratulations on finishing SOAR!

But we are not complete yet...

In a world saturated with noise and distractions, there is a constant seduction to fall back into old habits and beliefs, especially at the beginning of your transformational journey. Finding true alignment with your essence and rising to new heights of success can feel like an elusive dream.

I trust you can see that SOAR has introduced you to a transformational blueprint that is a fundamental foundation, with a multidisciplinary and holistic approach for your life. SOAR allows you to unlock your full potential. Remember, forward vision unlocks your potential. When you build your life on ancient wisdom, universal principles, and fundamental truths, the philosophies of ontology and metaphysics hold true, and you achieve results you could not even dream about yesterday.

But the journey does not end with the final chapter.

No, that's merely the beginning.

Envision a life where you are the architect of your destiny, liberated from the shackles of past limiting beliefs and behaviors. This is the promise of SOAR.

Gone are the days of feeling stuck in the same old patterns, endlessly repeating cycles of self-sabotage. I promise you that you will learn to navigate the labyrinth of life with purpose, focus, clarity, direction, and velocity. You will cultivate deep self-awareness, enabling you to transcend obstacles that once seemed insurmountable.

But perhaps most importantly, you will forge a profound connection with your essence, the core of your being. In this state of alignment, you will discover a reservoir of untapped power, ready to propel you toward fulfilling your dreams with unwavering certainty.

So why settle for a life confined by the limitations of the past when you can create your future and live your potential?

Take the first step towards your transformation today.

I offer several options to meet you where you are and support you on your journey. From personalized coaching to membership in the SOAR Institute for Holistic Living, where you will find valuable assets to help you on your journey.

Or transform your life by coupling SOAR with creating your Life Vision to Mastery! My 30-day, all-out, intensive, transformational, be the architect of your destiny, your life, and unlock your potential program.

If you are interested in this program, please email me at jim@omspiritualcenter.com. You may also check out more services and offers at **omspiritualcenter.com.**

I look forward to hearing from you.

To your SOARing success!

The SOAR Model

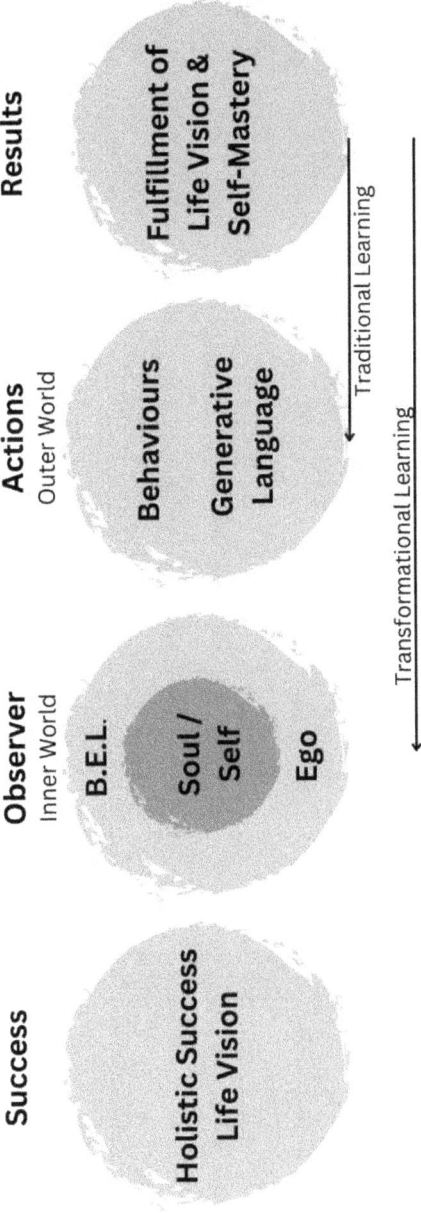

S.O.A.R.

Success

Holistic Success
Life Vision

Observer
Inner World

B.E.L.

Soul /
Self

Ego

Actions
Outer World

Behaviours
Generative
Language

Results

Fulfillment of
Life Vision &
Self-Mastery

Traditional Learning

Transformational Learning

www.ingramcontent.com/pod-product-compliance
Lightning Source LLC
Chambersburg PA
CBHW060013100426
42740CB00010B/1479